DRINKING IN COLLEGE

BY ROBERT STRAUS

MEDICAL CARE FOR SEAMEN

Drinking in College

ROBERT STRAUS AND SELDEN D. BACON

New Haven: Yale University Press, 1953

London: Geoffrey Cumberlege, Oxford University Press

BIP '86

ACKNOWLEDGMENTS

The survey was financed from the departmental budget of the Yale Laboratory of Applied Physiology and from part of a grant generously provided by I. Rogosin.

The authors are grateful to many persons for guidance, encouragement, and assistance in planning and carrying out the survey of drinking in college. The contributions of James G. March in the processing and analysis of data, and of Laura J. Barress and Priscilla B. Lettis as secretary-technicians, warrant special mention, along with the work of Betty J. Crowther, Richard O. Goodwillie, James G. Haden, Jennie Heiser, Ronald P. Karsel, Deborah S. Kligler, Kenneth E. Luther, Jr., George D. Malkasian, Jr., Alan K. McAdams, Frank M. McClain, and Beverly Rice. Valuable suggestions were made by Clements C. Fry, Howard W. Haggard, August B. Hollingshead, E. M. Jellinek, Mark Keller, Raymond G. McCarthy, Charles R. Snyder, and Fred L. Strodtbeck. Assistance in arranging or administering the survey was given by Joel Berreman, Vashti Ishee Cain, Ernest C. Campbell, John C. Ford, Katie Sue Echols, C. Wendell King, and Maurice L. Zigmond. Others assisting at various times were Genevieve Anderson, William Anderson, Myron Bell, Stanley D. Fons, Richard T. Hall, Hanni M. Holzman, Stanley I. Kilty, Chang Nai Kim, and John H. Koenig.

Expert help and guidance in publicity and public relations for the study were provided by Richard C. Lee and J. Richard Banks. Eugene Davidson and Mark Carroll contributed helpful editorial suggestions. We are particularly grateful to Roberta W. Yerkes

v

whose skillful editing of the entire manuscript has added greatly to the clarity of expression and organization.

To the presidents, deans, registrars, and faculty of the 27 participating colleges we are indebted for countless expressions of interest, cooperation, and kindness during the administration of the study. Our greatest debt is to the students whose intelligent and earnest responses to our questionnaire made the study possible.

CONTENTS

INTRODUCTION

This survey of the drinking customs and attitudes of a group of the college students in the United States was conceived as part of a larger study of the problems connected with alcohol in American society and their relationship to the custom of drinking, which has been under way for more than twenty years at the Laboratory of Applied Physiology and the Center of Alcohol Studies of Yale University. About 1930, scientists at the Laboratory began to specialize in the study of alcohol, especially on the effect of alcohol on the body and the effect of body functions upon alcohol. They soon realized that understanding of problems connected with alcoholic beverages could not be achieved through any single discipline. By the early 1940's the staff of the Laboratory had been gradually expanded to represent medicine, psychiatry, statistics, psychology, law, education, religion, and sociology. This wider orientation of research called for a more appropriate title, and the Center of Alcohol Studies emerged as a distinct part of the Laboratory.

For centuries, in societies all over the world, men and women have had to try to cope with various problems connected with alcoholic beverages. Today these appear in many forms from drunkenness, alcoholism, and the diseases of alcoholism, drinking and driving, loss of manpower and man hours, to legislation and enforcement of taxation, licensing, price, and other controls, the questions concerned with the training of youth, and the relation of drinking customs to other social problems. The program at the Center of Alcohol Studies has included research in all of these areas.

Since knowledge of facts alone can have only limited value without interpretation and application, the program of the center has

1

come to include the publication of a scientific journal and numerous books, monographs, and pamphlets; a diagnostic and research clinic for alcoholics; an annual summer institute providing
lectures, seminars, and discussion for specialists from the many
disciplines concerned with the problems of alcohol; the compila-
tion of an archive of abstracts of pertinent literature; and consulta-
tion services for industrial and business concerns, educational
groups, and government and community health agencies.

Studies of drinking customs are being approached according to
population groups based on such factors as ethnic or religious background or age. For example, studies are under way among first and
second generation Italians in America and among persons of Jewish faith. The survey of drinking in college deals with an age group
of particular significance, for these students are at the age when
drinking starts for many people. Because first experiences are fresh
in their minds it is easier for them than for older persons to identify
purposes, pressures, sanctions, and reactions associated with early
drinking.

The survey was initiated in 1947. A year and a half were devoted
to planning and the development of techniques. The actual col-
lection of data took place during 1949–51.

The study encompassed 27 colleges, selected to represent different types: public, private, and sectarian institutions; coeducational, men's, and women's; white and Negro; urban and rural;
with large and small enrollments; and in different regions of the
country.

It was agreed with administrators of the participating colleges
that the institutions would not be identified in the reports on the
survey; only categories of colleges would be considered. Geographically, the colleges were located as follows: 7 in New England, 2 in
the Middle Atlantic states, 6 South Atlantic, 3 East South Central,
3 East North Central, 1 West South Central, 3 Mountain, and 2
on the Pacific Coast. Eleven were tax-supported institutions and
16 privately controlled. Of the latter, 7 were nonsectarian and 9
controlled by various religious denominations. Two colleges in the
South were for Negroes only, and one of the northern schools included a sizable Negro enrollment. One college had under 500
students, 6 had from 500 to 1,000, 5 from 1,000 to 2,000, 2 from

2,000 to 3,000, 4 from 3,000 to 4,000, 3 from 4,000 to 5,000, and 6 had more than 5,000 students. Twenty of the colleges were co-educational, 5 were for men and 2 for women only. Five were located in metropolitan areas (over 200,000 population), 8 in smaller urban areas, 3 in suburban districts, 9 in small towns (2,500–25,000 population), and 2 in rural areas.

Within each college a sample was obtained for the survey by selecting class groups which approximated the total student body with respect to distribution according to sex, college year, and major field of study. While the participants represent the total enrollment of the 27 particular colleges they do not necessarily represent all segments of American college youth. In particular, they include, quite intentionally, a somewhat disproportionately large number of Mormon and Jewish students. These cultural groups were selected for special study because they have unique sanctions with respect to drinking which are of particular significance. The use of alcoholic beverages in moderation has deep symbolic meaning and is widespread among Jews, while all drinking is rigidly prohibited by Mormon codes. In this report, Mormons are referred to as a religious group distinct from other Protestants.

The principal technique employed in the survey was a questionnaire. This was supplemented by discussions with students, faculty members, and administrators, and by general observations made at each college by members of the survey staff. Questionnaires were administered to 17,000 students. Seven hundred of these participated in a series of pretests: small groups of students filled out preliminary questionnaire forms and then gave considerable time to discussing the content, wording, and set-up of each question. By this means it was possible to eliminate ambiguous or irrelevant questions, to develop definitions which had meaning in terms of student behavior and student vernacular, and, for some questions, to develop check lists of the most frequent types of response, which facilitated the coding of data for machine tabulation. Items included in the final questionnaire are listed in the Appendix. Of the 16,300 students who filled out the final versions of the questionnaire, the responses of 15,747 or 96.6% have been used in this analysis. This very high rate of usable returns is evidence of the intelligent, sincere, and rather serious spirit of cooperation with which the vast majority of the students met the survey. Each questionnaire was examined for responses which suggested insincerity. There were also explicit tests for consistency, by comparing the responses to several sets of closely related questions presented in different contexts and in different parts of the questionnaire. Among those rejected were about 250 students whose systematic inconsistency suggested either lack of understanding or lack of interest, about 100 visiting foreign students who could not be considered as representative of American college youth and who were often handicapped by language difficulties, and about 100 students who made sarcastic or humorous responses. Most of the latter were male students from one school where a member of the faculty assisting with the distribution of the forms invited attempts at humor with a joking remark at the start.

The questionnaires, which were designed to take about 40 minutes to complete, were administered to organized class groups during regular class hours,[1] without previous announcement. Students who did not care to participate were excused; very rarely did any leave. A few written directions were included on the questionnaire. In addition a brief and standardized oral explanation was provided by the survey staff, who described the survey's relationship to a number of social problems, the need for facts to replace speculation about the drinking customs of college students, and the hope that the study might provide a basis for more realistic understanding and action by all concerned. Every attempt was made in this introduction to be straight-forward, to indicate respect for the students' experience and opinions, and to convey the confidence that they would respond in kind. They were presented with a serious group of questions in a manner which indicated respect for their intelligence and integrity. We can report that an overwhelming majority showed themselves deserving of this respect.

Whether they drink or abstain, young people cannot avoid personal decisions and conflicts regarding the use of alcoholic beverages. For such reasons as these most of the students were interested in the subject and in the survey. They asked questions at every opportunity about the survey or about various problems hav-

1. In a few instances several groups of students were brought together in a large hall. At three of the smaller colleges the whole student body participated.

ing to do with alcohol. A further indication of their acceptance of
the survey and its purposes was their willingness to cooperate in
a follow-up study. No names appeared on the questionnaires, but
each form contained a separate insert sheet numbered to correspond with the study number on the form. Students were asked if
they were willing to sign these separate sheets so that later follow-up
studies might be made. They were assured that these sheets would
be kept under lock and key, separate from the questionnaires, and
would be available solely to the survey directors, for use only in
selecting a sample for further study. Seventy-seven per cent of the
students (76% of the men and 81% of the women) felt sufficiently
interested and secure to comply—a surprisingly high and very
significant percentage.

It is of course not possible to measure the exact degree of accuracy of information provided by the students. Any research
technique has certain limitations, and the printed questionnaire
is no exception. There is always the possibility that the choice of
words or the order of questions or their arrangement on the page
will in some way bias the responses. The introductory explanation,
the presence or absence of certain persons, or other circumstances
connected with the presentation of the questionnaires may also
influence replies. For some questions, such as family income or
drinking practices of parents, we must assume variation in the students' knowledge or perception. Other items which deal with personal feelings or opinions must be interpreted as the subjective
type of information which they are. Even questions about measurable facts, such as frequency of drinking, amounts usually consumed, or number of times intoxicated, depend on memory and
on other factors of perception which can vary tremendously from
individual to individual.

While it must be remembered that our data are necessarily subject to the limitations of individual perception, we have attempted,
with the experience gained through our pretests, to minimize bias
or confusion. The high degree of consistency found in the majority
of the questionnaires, and the attitude of the students as expressed
in their statements indicate that the participants in this study, with
very few exceptions, were trying to provide us with accurate information.

Most of the data of the study were coded and punched on machine tabulation cards. Certain of the more intricate operations which involved many cards for each individual were conducted with a 10 per cent sample of the participants, selected by picking the questionnaires with identifying numbers ending in the digit 5. The validity of the 10 per cent sample was tested by comparing it with the whole according to the distribution of responses on all basic data. Most variations were confined to fractions of percentage points. With a few exceptions the discussion in Chapters 8, 11, 12, and 14 is based on the 10 per cent sample (1,047 men and 521 women), while other chapters are based largely on the total group of participants (10,526 men and 5,221 women).

One of the key problems in analyzing and presenting highly complicated quantitative data is to find a mode of presentation which makes understanding easy without leading to oversimplification or distortion. To keep the reader from being lost in the maze of tabulations and computations which are the basis of our analysis, we have presented all findings in percentages, thus avoiding confusing variations in numerical frequencies. We have not burdened our pages with repeated measures of probability for errors due to chance.[2] In only a few instances where special devices were employed does a technical measure of significance appear. While a more detailed technical presentation is of course desirable for those who are expert in statistics, a nontechnical presentation is useful from the viewpoint of the general reader.

In addition to eliminating much prevailing speculation about the specific subject of drinking in college, the survey brings out certain basic facts about the nature and onset of the drinking custom in American society, and should have application to some of the problems of alcohol relating to all young people. It is hoped that its findings may contribute to better understanding of behavior in the whole area, as well as suggest a basis for more reasonable and realistic action by parents, teachers, religious leaders, judges, physicians, public health authorities, and others who are called upon to make important decisions and provide guidance with respect to drinking; that they may aid teachers, administra-

2. The X^2 test at the .01 level of probability was used as a criterion of significance.

tors, and mental health authorities in developing programs of alcohol education, in dealing with disciplinary problems, and in working with psychological and medical problems in which drinking is an associated factor; and that they may contribute to the health and emotional well-being of college students themselves by providing insights into the nature of drinking customs and, for those who prefer to abstain, a rationale satisfactory to themselves and their associates.

More important perhaps than its immediate findings is the possibility that this survey will help to identify pertinent questions which can be subjected in the future to more rigorous and intensive research techniques.

CHAPTER 1. *American Drinking:*

Controversies and Problems

The drinking of alcoholic beverages in the United States has been blessed and cursed, has been held the cause of economic catastrophe and the hope for prosperity, the major cause of crime, disease, military defeat, and depravity and a sign of high prestige, mature personality, and a refined civilization. These varying opinions have been expressed in our courts, our churches, our colleges, newspapers, legislatures, clubs, and homes. Drinking has been discussed sometimes with insight, sometimes with emotion, by jurists, industrialists, politicians, novelists, playwrights and poets, physicians, clergymen, teachers, and parents. For more than a century the subject has been of insistent and vocal concern to our society, perhaps surpassed in frequency of discussion only by money and sex.

Opinions about drinking have been expressed in literally hundreds of thousands of books, articles, editorials, sermons, judicial and legislative decisions, advertisements, comic strips, moving pictures, texts and tracts. This profusion of argument and assertion is in striking contrast to facts about drinking in the United States —which are almost nonexistent. Who drinks, what, when, where, how much, how often, starting at what age, with whom, with what satisfactions or ill effects, with what beliefs, under what influences to drink or abstain? These and many other questions have not been answered. They have seldom even been asked.

It is not difficult to account for the continued outpouring of emotion and assertion about drinking. Very real and painful problems are associated with the use of alcohol. Very real satisfactions also attend its use. Furthermore, the custom of drinking is widespread in our society. Probably between 60 and 80 million people in this country drink alcoholic beverages in some form, out of a total population of about 108 million (past the age of 15).

The problems and satisfactions associated with drinking are rarely discussed together. One aspect or the other holds attention; and when occasionally the other is mentioned it is usually as a straw man marked for immediate destruction. From the vantage point of systematic study, however, both problems and satisfactions stem from one process: the depressant action of alcohol, which increases with intake. The word "depressant" covers reduction in speed of reaction, in ability to discriminate, and in exercise of control over behavior—especially behavior that has been learned with difficulty, learned in opposition to individual desire, or learned recently. Following a brief increase in sensory acuity with small amounts, sensitivity to light, sound, taste, and odor is also reduced.

The outstanding effect of drinking is the reduction in discrimination and the consequent loss of judgment and control. True, many of the ordinary situations of life require no high degree of discrimination, physical sensitivity, or speed in reaction time. It was once brought out, at a Congressional hearing on the intoxicating qualities of beer, that if a man drank one bottle before breakfast it would so affect his reflexes as to make it dangerous for him to try to walk a tightrope. The question was immediately raised, not entirely flippantly, as to what sort of man would wish to walk a tightrope before breakfast. But that alcohol reduces nervous and muscular efficiency has been clearly shown on the firing range and in tests of typewriting, of using sewing machines, and the like. Such loss in mechanical efficiency is of obvious importance for example in operating a car.

Of even greater importance is the effect of alcohol on learned behavior, and especially on self-evaluation and self-control. If an individual has "learned" through childhood and adolescence that he is inadequate or inferior, if he has learned that he cannot compete successfully with others, alcohol may serve temporarily to reduce the pain of the knowledge. All individuals have to learn to respect the rights of others, to limit their aggressive and exhibitionistic and selfish impulses. As any parent knows, this learning is not automatic and easy. Nor do the motivations for aggression or aggrandizement disappear. Sometimes the desire to "tell off" the boss, to appear as the life of the party, or to indulge in self-pity is very close to the surface indeed. The learned controls then should come into play. This hard-won learning is quickly dulled by alcohol. Shyness, caution, modesty, reserve, sharing, giving way to others, and restraining aggressive impulses are temporarily subjected to unlearning under alcohol. Sometimes this is regarded as beneficial; if someone has "overlearned" these controls, his friends may feel a little alcohol improves his personality.

A comment should be added about the drinker's perception, discrimination, and judgment in relation to his own behavior after drinking. He may well feel that he is acting more efficiently than usual. Self-criticism is a painfully learned process at best, and with alcohol is quickly dulled. Moreover, if the individual is one of those who appears to have overlearned individual controls, he may have cast off, in drinking, some of his social liabilities. But unfortunately alcohol plays no favorites in its depressant functioning, and he may also lose some of his social assets. His own perception of this at the time will be dull. Later he may be overly self-critical or overly self-congratulatory. There are those who feel that they drive a car more carefully after several drinks than when completely sober, and who point to the fact that while they never drive under 45 miles an hour when sober they never exceed 25 after drinks. Even when this appears to be true, however, they may drive carefully through red lights at 25 miles an hour or steadily and cautiously hug the wrong side of the road. Subjective judgments on "how alcohol affects me," whether before, during, or after drinking, are consistently unreliable.

Small amounts of alcohol have the same type of effect as larger amounts, but when the situation does not call for marked sensitivity, speed of reaction, discrimination, and self-control no untoward effects are noted. As the amount increases, untoward effects become obvious unless the situation calls for less of these qualities. It is not surprising that the proponents of drinking usually refer to consuming small amounts of alcohol in situations of casual relaxation at the end of the day, while the opponents consider large amounts with reference to athletes or to those about to operate a 2,000-pound mechanism at high speed on a crowded highway.

The same division may be seen in relation to discussions of sensitivity, reaction speed, discrimination, and control. The advocates of drinking note that the process of aging is accompanied by a variety of aches and irritations; no modern miracle drugs have been found to conquer old age. But sensitivity to these painful stimuli is temporarily reduced by small amounts of alcohol. Similarly, the advocates point out that in our complex, interdependent, competitive, and often insecure society many people are burdened with extreme anxieties and self-controls and live at a hectic tempo. Necessary or effective though this may be for peak production, it may be destructive of emotional satisfactions and interpersonal relationships; it may even diminish effectiveness in peak production. Small amounts of alcohol serve to reduce this tension, allay anxiety, and open the way for more meaningful and effective personal relations. The opponents observe drinking by young people; the loss of judgment, self-control, and the respect of others that may ensue; the lowering of standards in their relations with one another; and the physical damage to self, property, and other people. Sometimes it is hard to believe that the opponents and advocates are talking about the same subject.

From the depressant action of alcohol arise the pleasures and pains which explain both the use of alcoholic beverages and the attacks and defenses of that use. There is a wide variety of secondary reasons for drinking—to keep warm, to cool off; to "pep up," to relax; to enjoy taste or odor, benefit by food value or medicinal value; to copy others; to obtain aesthetic satisfaction or comply with religious ceremonial, and so on—but these are clearly not of first importance either in adopting or in keeping up the custom of drinking. The secondary reasons for attacking and defending the use of alcohol are more apparent and perhaps more important than the secondary reasons for drinking. They concern profits, revenue from taxes, maintenance of organizations directly involved in controversy about alcohol, or membership in organizations traditionally accepting positive or negative viewpoints about drinking as part of a larger program, and so forth. But if the depressant effect of alcohol were eliminated, drinking, together with the attacks upon it would shortly disappear.

The point of origin for almost all the literature and argument, whether pro or con, is the problems associated with drinking. The arguments, however, have been developed over such a long period, with such fervor, and under the guidance of such well-organized groups, that they often appear to have a life of their own independent of their source. On occasion controversies rage about issues which may appear quite remote to members of the public who may be concerned about drinking but are not aware of what might be called the party lines. For example, in 1953 two issues, the lowering of federal taxes on alcoholic beverages and the control of their advertising, clearly dominated the minds of Wets and Drys. For many persons it is not easy to see how victory or defeat on one issue or the other for either of the contestants would in any way affect the basic problems. We shall classify the problems in order to give the reader a vantage point from which to view these conflicts and decide without benefit of party lines what is more and what is less significant for a better understanding of drinking problems in our society.

One type of problem emerges directly from drinking which is generally regarded as excessive for the situation. It is not the drinking itself, of course, but the associated or consequent behavior of the drinker, behavior lacking control or discrimination, which forces recognition of a problem. Drunkenness is the chief example in this category. Another example, one often involving far less consumption of alcohol, is drunken driving. Chronic drunkenness forms a third example, alcoholism a fourth. In all of these cases the problem is immediately and directly related to the individual's consumption of alcohol.

Other people are also affected by the behavior of the drinker. Some of them are obviously upset or directly injured by uncontrolled behavior, as is the family that finds a drunk lying on the front lawn, the bystander who is killed by an intoxicated driver, or the host whose china is smashed. However, the impact is often less immediate. The family of the alcoholic, the administrators and faculty of a school or college in which a drinking scandal takes place, the business associates of a man whose drunken behavior involves his firm, these and many others more or less removed from the scene may suffer greatly. They too are victims of excessive drinking, but in a different sense from the alcoholics, the chronic drunkards, or the individual who once had too much.

A third and decidedly different sort of irritant may be termed the derived as distinct from the direct problem. No society can long tolerate uncontrolled, insensitive, and inadequate behavior. If such behavior increases and can be identified, societal reaction is called for. As people live closer together geographically and become more interdependent (often without knowing each other), and as conditions of life grow less secure, the need for sensitive, discriminating, and controlled behavior becomes greater. Fires increase because wooden houses are built close together; disease spreads with the unregulated sinking of wells and sewers; accidents multiply as more and faster vehicles appear on narrow, rough streets. Society has to react. The reaction almost always involves the loss of previous individual rights and the imposition of new individual responsibilities. In achieving the new adjustment, the society often goes through a good deal of conflict; individuals rarely welcome new responsibilities and invariably dislike giving up former rights or privileges. In the instances mentioned, however, building codes and sanitary laws and traffic control were developed and, within two or three generations, became rather generally accepted.

Such new adjustment and general acceptance has not taken place insofar as the direct problems associated with excessive drinking are concerned. Nor have the problems disappeared. Two consequences of this may be noted: there are conflicts about what ought to be done, and "something," whether effective in the long run or not, *has* to be done—one cannot disregard the drunk, the drunken driver, or the alcoholic.

The seriousness of this type of derived problem can hardly be overemphasized. Differing conceptions of what ought or ought not to be done about alcohol have cost our society untold amounts of intellectual, spiritual, and material capital for more than a century. The conflict about what should be done may well have cost more than the original direct problem. Some examples may illustrate the extent and the intensity of this derived social problem.

American church groups are in sharp disagreement, sometimes in open conflict, as to both the nature of the problem and what should be done about it. Although all agree that drunkenness is a problem, many feel that the real difficulty is drinking and that abstinence, whether achieved by persuasion or force, is the only answer. Over 40 million Americans belong to church groups that hold the latter belief. About an equal number belong to sects holding other views. There are groups within the sects on both sides which disagree with the stand taken by the majority: there are total abstinence groups in churches which do not stand for total abstinence; there are "moderation" groups in churches which stand for total abstinence. Nor do the conflict and confusion stop at this point. There are individual churches which clearly fail to adhere to the denominational policy. Perhaps most significant of all, large numbers of individual members of total abstinence churches, who otherwise accept their religion and participate in its activities, reject their church's policy on this matter in thought or action, sometimes quite openly. There are also members of churches with what might be called a moderation policy who feel strongly that their church's policy is weak and wrong. Major denominations have formally changed their policies in the last decade. Others are considering changes, some of a peripheral nature, some involving the core of their philosophy. Bitter antagonisms have even flared openly at formal gatherings.

On the political level the conflict and confusion achieved a dramatic peak in the first third of this century with two formal changes of the Constitution. However, the political conflict neither began nor ended with these constitutional amendments. From the earliest days of settlement to the present moment towns, cities, counties, and states have fought the battle of "what should be done." Prohibition first appeared in colonial days, and groups of states tried it at three different times between 1840 and 1920. Local option contests occur the country over year after year. The struggle is not merely over prohibition, state monopoly, or license systems on a legislative level. All sorts of executive and administrative boards and judicial bodies manifest the confusion and conflict.

The problem is seen in sanitary codes, zoning regulations, traffic laws, educational requirements, welfare and penal legislation, medical administration, supervision of federal wards, maritime jurisdictions, military activities, veterans affairs; even budgets for diplomats reflect the conflict. What many persons believe to have been the most powerful political party machine ever developed in the United States on the national level, the model for all others in this century, was concerned not with war or taxes, unions or depressions, communism or fascism, but with liquor. This was the Anti-Saloon League, organized in 1895, which within twenty years had achieved a position perhaps never matched in our political history.

One other example, especially pertinent to this book, is the confusion reigning in the field of education. Every state in the Union has legislation directing the public schools to teach pupils about alcohol; often the law specifies that the teaching is to be about the evils of alcohol. At first glance this might seem to refute the assertion of conflict and confusion. It would have to be a brief glance indeed to leave such an impression. Although this is perhaps the only specific educational requirement to be found the country over, confusion and conflict are compounded in it. The legal requirement is often complied with by bringing in persons not members of the school staff or not even members of the teaching profession, who utilize materials not prepared by professional educators, and whose message is never integrated with the curriculum. The materials have often been at variance in content, method, and orientation with even minimum educational standards. Many teachers and superintendents refuse to teach what the law requires because of personal feelings, the religious and social attitudes of the students and their parents, or broad community pressures. How effective educational efforts have been with the segment of the population studied in this book we shall see later.

These examples are cited to indicate the breakdown of individual and social integration or morality which is intimately associated with the programs for meeting the problems of alcohol. Incompatible programs have been sources of conflict for generations; and the conflict has spread to groups, social institutions, and individual lives. It has become entangled with other major problems—

religious, racial, legal, educational, medical—and has added to
their force, while they have lent some of their socially disintegrat-
ing power to the problems of drinking. The conflict over what
ought or ought not to be done may well be the major social problem rising from the use of alcoholic beverages.

Whether or not the activities of the groups with organized programs have been effective in combatting the direct problems, one
fact remains undeniable: the problems are still with us. Because
the meaning of the terms used in records of 100 or 50 or even 25
years ago is uncertain, because we do not know what proportion of
cases were reported, and because even the validity of such records
as exist is open to serious question, it is not possible to state that
this or that problem was greater or lesser in 1850 or 1900 or 1950—
except in such instances as industrial or automobile accidents. Even
here the figures available in 1953 are of small value. Usually there is
no record. When probable instances occur there is no way to
verify the fact, and small desire to find out; objection to such attempts is common. However, there is little question that the number of alcoholics (by any definition) runs into millions; that annual
fatalities in automobile accidents alone, where alcohol is involved,
exceed our annual deaths in the Korean war; and that our jails and
workhouses the country over exist primarily for the temporary
restraint of those found guilty of drunkenness. Despite the lack of
agreement on what should be done and the popular response of
doing nothing (to be discussed in the following chapter), it is almost impossible to avoid action when uncontrolled behavior following excessive drinking threatens or literally smashes the ordinary securities of life. To the majority of the public, arguments
about excise taxes and advertisements appear somewhat esoteric
in these instances.

The second type of derived problems concerns these necessary
actions. As would be expected, lack of agreement as to what should
be done leads to all sorts of incompatible actions. As would also
be expected, none of the actions is particularly successful. Some
police departments arrest all drunks, others arrest only the worst
cases. Some present many of those arrested for drunkenness to the
court; others present less than a third. Some courts use suspended

sentences in most of the cases presented; some are prone to hand out long jail sentences. Among the clergy some have recourse to exhortation, prayer, and pledges; others turn to Alcoholics Anonymous, counseling, and clinics; still others use threats. Employers, parents, husbands or wives, and friends try a multitude of responses: firing, cursing, pity, love, medical treatments, sanitaria, travel, and, above all, hiding the situation as long as possible. Hospitals, social agencies, and physicians avoid the problem whenever possible, turning to missions, police, commitment to mental hospitals, and the like. These last get rid of the cases as they can, their turnover of repeaters being enormous. Almost any police department in a city of 100,000 or more can point to individuals with records of more than 200 arrests on the one count of drunkenness.

The problems of what to do about alcohol and how to do it face many organizations and many individuals. The most dramatic situations, of course, are met by those who cannot avoid the impact or ignore the responsibility. Their technical tasks are always made more difficult by the ignorance, stigma, and conflict surrounding the larger isue. Questions of technique also are faced by the organized Wets and Drys: what issues to select for attack; what types of progaganda to use; how to build their own organizations and develop new allies. Questions of technique are presented to enforcement and revenue agents, to educators, to research workers and medical men, to insurance companies and foundations, to personnel officers and politicians.

Last but not least are the parents of adolescent children; to whom can they delegate the task of guidance and leadership? Should Johnnie or Susan at sixteen drink beer, cocktails, sherry? Should they drink at night clubs, or only at home? Is such drinking dangerous? Should they go around with boys and girls who drink? What should one tell them? Will they accept negative advice? If they do accept it, will they lose friends, be irritated or hypocritical with their parents, start drinking at greater risk three or four years later? In back of all these questions lie the disagreements and uncertainties that characterize religion, education, government, medicine, and society in general in relation to the use of alcohol.

This classification of problems is an attempt to clear away some

of the confusion surrounding the subject of drinking. Since what
raises the issues is not usually drinking but the problems associated
with excessive drinking, it is evident that much of the controversy
is taking place on different levels and is conducted by persons
facing different problems or defining similar problems in very
different fashion. This may help to explain why certain of the
groups trying to do something about alcohol oppose each other
or consider each other's interests or actions irrelevant. Members
of Alcoholics Anonymous, the Woman's Christian Temperance
Union, police departments, psychiatrists, traffic court judges, college authorities, alcoholic beverage control boards, and the leaders
of a "moderation" Protestant denomination may all wish "to do
something" and may even be doing it. Yet they may fail to see anything of value in each other's programs, may actively oppose them,
or merely disapprove what detracts from support which might have
come to them. Sometimes they disagree with one another's definition of the problem, sometimes with the particular aspects selected
for attack, sometimes only with the tactics. To the public this confusion and conflict between the interested parties makes an already
murky picture even more blurred and disconcerting.

Much of the controversy and much of the confusion can be traced
directly to lack of facts. The problem aspects of drinking can only
be understood within the larger framework of knowledge about
drinking. One who set himself up to be an expert on earthquakes
without any knowledge of the structure of the earthcrust would
be considered a fool. One who wished to be an expert on liver
disease but refused to study the structure and functioning of the
liver would be thought a quack. In relation to problems of drinking, however, whether one be a minister, teacher, judge, physician,
or legislator, it is apparently assumed that knowledge of the phenomenon which is causing trouble is unnecessary, and that all one
needs is the will to attack it. But this approach has proven ineffective over more than a century of earnest, organized effort, enormous
financial investment, and leadership which can readily be termed
inspired. Knowledge of their nature and size and position may not
by itself solve problems, but absence of knowledge can almost
guarantee failure.

The description to be presented in this book of the drinking habits and attitudes of a single segment of our population is offered as one step toward that knowledge. Before these facts are presented, however, something more than a statement about problems and controversies connected with drinking is required: some picture is needed of the drinking habits and attitudes of the whole society within which this segment, the college population, lives.

CHAPTER 2. *Drinking Customs and Attitudes in American Society* [1]

Habits and attitudes do not rise fully formed out of thin air; nor, contrary to a good deal of popular opinion, do they appear as a result of single events or the wise words of a great leader. Rather they emerge through generations of trial and error, out of the forms of behavior, theories, organizations, and needs of the surrounding society. American drinking customs and beliefs are no exception to this rule. They were brought to this country by the first settlers, and have been affected here by changing political, religious, economic, military, philosophical, and other factors. Later immigrants from different countries have brought with them their own customs and attitudes toward alcoholic beverages, some of them very different from the ways of the first settlers.

Knowledge of the drinking habits and attitudes of past centuries is limited. Some information can be gleaned from laws, recipe books, tax records, religious and government reports, travelers'

1. Data for this chapter have been drawn primarily from the following sources: E. G. Baird, "The Alcohol Problem and the Law," Pt. 2, "The Common-Law Basis of Modern Liquor Controls," *Quarterly Journal of Studies on Alcohol,* 5 (June 1944), 120–161 (quotation from p. 148); H. W. Haggard and E. M. Jellinek, *Alcohol Explored* (Garden City, Doubleday, Doran, 1945); E. M. Jellinek, "Recent Trends in Alcoholism and in Alcohol Consumption," *Quarterly Journal of Studies on Alcohol,* 8 (June 1947), 1–42 (quotation from p. 9); R. G. McCarthy and E. M. Douglass, *Alcohol and Social Responsibility* (New York, Thomas Y. Crowell, 1949; quotation from pp. 20–21). Statistics on consumption were compiled by M. Keller and V. Efron of the Yale Center of Alcohol Studies.

comment, diaries, or the work of writers and artists. Although no single source can be relied upon for an over-all picture and although the scope, accuracy, viewpoint and use of terms in these reports show great variation, the major facts and trends are fairly clear. As a background for considering the present drinking practices of American college students we shall attempt to review briefly the origins and development of drinking customs in American society. We are concerned with trends in two areas: patterns of consumption of alcoholic beverages and certain significant forms of social response to these customs.

Patterns of Consumption

The colonists who came here from England brought with them a constellation of habits and attitudes relating to the use of alcohol. Alcoholic beverages had religious, medical, dietary, recreational, and commercial significance for them. Beer, wine, and distilled spirits were all known and used, although spirits, which only became generally available after 1500, may not have been consumed very widely or frequently. Drinking, at the time of settlement, was largely confined to beer and wines.

During the 18th and early 19th centuries the distilling industry gained an important place in the economy both of England and America. The brewing industry was already well established in the home country but had not taken root in the colonies. The rise of distilling here served to check a growth that might otherwise have occurred in brewing and the consumption of beer, thus contributing to the development of different drinking patterns in England and the colonies. The manufacture of distilled spirits was economically attractive because they were much less bulky to transport than the grain from which they came or than beer. Spoilage of grain shipments, too, in days of slow and uncertain transportation was another factor that favored distillation. And even more important in the economy than grain distilling was the triangular trade in molasses, slaves, and rum.

Some idea of the consumption of alcohol in the early days of the republic can be gained from the fact that recorded imports of spirits in the 1790's approximated a gallon a year for every man, woman, and child. And in 1807, it is recorded, Boston had 40 distilleries, one for every 625 persons—but only 2 breweries. There were continual attempts during the 18th century to develop the brewing industry, but it could not compete successfully with the distilling business in the economy of that period. Much higher transportation costs in relation to alcohol content and price were a handicapping factor (a distinction plain to bootleggers of the Prohibition era of 1919–33). The domestic wine industry was of little importance and high costs of importation placed wine beyond the means of most people.

The relative use of distilled drinks increased steadily from early colonial times. During the first half of the 19th century about 90% of the alcohol consumed in this country was in the form of distilled spirits, perhaps 6% beer and 4% wine. But about 1840 a sharp reversal of this trend began, although the per capita consumption of absolute alcohol varied only slightly. By the 1890's the amount of alcohol consumed in spirits had fallen below that consumed in beer. This trend has continued, and in 1950 distilled spirits contributed only 40% of the total alcohol consumption, beer 49%, and wine 11%. Per capita consumption of spirits (for those 15 and over) dropped from 4.17 gallons in 1850 to 1.72 in 1950, while for beer in the same period it rose from 2.70 gallons to 23.21 and for wine from 0.46 to 1.27.

This dramatic shift in types of alcoholic beverage consumed is significant in terms of effects on behavior. Given amounts of alcohol consumed as beer will have quite different effects from the same amount of alcohol in the form of whisky. Drink for drink, naturally, the latter is many times more powerful. There is a quart of alcohol in two quarts of bonded whisky—or in nearly 25 quarts of beer. Since the first amount is within the range of possible daily fluid consumption and the second far beyond it, it is clear that the concentrations of alcohol in the body and the subsequent effects will be quite different in beer drinking and in whisky drinking societies.

Changes in consumption after 1840 were associated with marked changes in the composition of the population. Before the American Revolution over 90% of the white population were of British antecedents. Of the more than 39 million persons who have migrated to the United States since 1820 more than half came from southern, central, and eastern Europe where the beverages used are predominantly brewed or fermented.

Some indication of the impact of this non-English immigration on total American consumption can be seen by comparing the beverages used in the South with use in other parts of the country. Almost none of the immigrants from southern, central, or eastern Europe moved into the South. The southern states have not experienced the same degree of change from distilled spirits to beer as the rest of the country, and still consume much more alcohol in the form of distilled spirits than as beer. In 1950 in 5 southern states (Alabama, Arkansas, Florida, Georgia, South Carolina) spirits contributed from 51 to 66% of the total legal alcohol consumption, and beer from 30 to 38%. In most other states more alcohol is consumed in beer than in spirits. In 1950 in 6 northern states (Massachusetts, New York, Ohio, Oregon, Pennsylvania, Wisconsin) spirits contributed from 29 to 41% of total legal alcohol consumption, beer from 48 to 61%. Since illegal production of distilled spirits has been centered in the southern states, except during national Prohibition, the actual difference between southern consumption and that in the rest of the country is even greater than official records suggest.

The 19th-century immigrants, besides furnishing a ready-made market for the brewing industry, included experienced brewers with sound technical knowledge. And the trend toward urbanization, by providing large concentrations of population in small areas, created more favorable conditions for the brewing business, for costly long-distance hauls to market were no longer necessary.

Changes in the types of beverage consumed have been accompanied by shifts in other patterns of drinking, including number of people who drink and the amounts they consume. In the United States today, as compared with a hundred years ago, more persons use alcoholic beverages but the average consumption per user is much less. For the century ending in 1950 (less the years of national Prohibition) the records reveal only slight fluctuations in absolute alcohol consumption; the figure in 1850 was 2.07 gallons per capita for everyone 15 years old and over; in 1950 it was 2.04 gallons. But as Jellinek has noted, "a large consumption of distilled spirits and a small consumption of beer is generally an indication that

the users are relatively few in number but individually heavy con-
sumers. A large consumption of beer, on the other hand, is indicative of wide use and relatively small individual consumption. The
fact that the consumption of distilled spirits in 1850 was 4.17 gallons per capita . . . while the per capita consumption of beer
was only 2.70 gallons would indicate that at that time few were
moderate drinkers, but that the division was largely between heavy
drinkers and abstainers." Various estimates place the present number of drinkers at about 65% of the adult population, divided to
include roughly 75% of the men and 55% of the women. Since
the number of users in the last century has increased while absolute
alcohol consumption remained fairly level, it follows that per capita
consumption for users has declined markedly.

The changes between 1600 and the present in the types of beverage consumed have also been accompanied by changes in the place
of drinking and in the kinds of users. Before 1700 drinking occurred primarily in the home, and both men and women used
the beers and wines which were the predominant beverages of the
times. During the next 150 years not only did distilled spirits come
to displace beer and wine but the tavern, especially in the business
section of the city and on the frontier, came to be the place of drinking. In early colonial days the tavern, besides serving the needs of
travelers, had been a center of community life, and its keeper ful-
filled an important role in community leadership. By the 19th
century, however, taverns had become primarily centers of all-male
recreation in which drinking held the chief place; and the once
respected tavern keeper often had been succeeded by the sometimes disreputable saloonkeeper.

In the 20th century, with the marked decline in drinking of distilled spirits and the tenfold increase in the use of beer everywhere
but in the South, there has been a decrease in the importance of
the commercial drinking establishment and an increase in drinking in the home. At the same time drinking by women has also
shown a marked increase. A sign of this change is the fact that
while beer was once sold primarily from the tap in the tavern
about 70% of it is now sold in the grocery or package store, most
of it certainly for use in the home.

A 19th-century development, significant here chiefly because of the response which it inspired, was the emergence of what may be called frontier drinking. This term describes the boisterous, heavy drinking that was most characteristic of places where there were young, single, adventurous men far removed from the controls of family, neighborhood, church, and other stabilizing influences. Reports of such wild drinking, often accompanied by brutal or violent behavior, go back to the time of the Revolution. Contemporary novels, accounts of travelers, and many other sources describe instances of such behavior among the Mississippi River boatmen, the men of the cattle and mining towns in the 1870's and 80's, and in the California and Alaska gold rushes. In situations of this sort where opportunities for recreation were scarce and limited, drinking was one of the few pastimes available. Reports suggest that the conquest of the continent was quite regularly accompanied by the drinking of distilled spirits.

Following close behind the hard-drinking, relatively lawless and unrestrained frontiersmen came the families of settlers. Communities were established, with churches and schools; property ownership appeared, and neighborhood life. These institutions were incompatible with the ways of the frontier, and could not accept them. Excessive drinking along with its center, the bar or saloon, began to become a symbol of the forces opposed to civilization, progress, and the solidarity of the home. To those families who were gradually filling up the country behind the westward-moving frontier the word drinking came to mean the brutish swilling of whisky accompanied by gambling, fighting, and immorality.

The pattern of behavior described as frontier drinking was not necessarily limited to the frontiers. A similar pattern developed in many of the swiftly growing cities during this period. Crowded housing, lack of recreational facilities, the rush of single men to the cities, the development of a new wage-earning class, and the social and moral disintegration associated with rapid growth were accompanied by an increase in heavy drinking and the development of taverns of "low repute."

It should be stressed that while these developments were taking place the more stable elements of society, especially in the older, urban regions of the eastern seaboard, retained their traditions of drinking beer, wine, and moderate amounts of spirits, in the home or tavern. Some of the inns and taverns used by travelers continued to be famous for their meals, furnishings, and service, as well as for their alcoholic beverages.

Frontier life was little more than an exciting memory by 1920; and the cities, though they had hardly achieved Utopian status, showed both slower rates of growth and increasingly effective adaptation in health provisions, housing, recreation, education, and so on, to the needs of their population. The social disorganization of city life, especially as it was evidenced in excessive and depraved drinking, has been vastly reduced both in intensity and in extent during the past hundred years. Yet though they have practically disappeared, frontier drinking and its urban counterpart of the 19th century should not be underestimated as influences on patterns of drinking and attitudes about drinking in the mid-20th century. The stigma associated with them was readily generalized to apply to all drinking, which became repulsive to the stabler elements in society and was seen as a threat to the family, church, community, and to morality in general. As we shall see, despite the fact that the customs themselves have shown remarkable change, the attitudes stemming from this 19th-century experience have continued to influence programs of action and beliefs about drinking and the problems of alcohol.

Social Responses to Drinking

The colonists when they came to these shores brought with them full awareness of the problems of drunkenness and the need to maintain adequate controls over the manufacture and sale of alcohol. They brought deep-seated family sanctions against excessive drinking. Their religious leaders strongly stated the evils of excess although they left the administration of formal controls to the political authorities. Drunkenness was considered a serious matter but not evidence of any intrinsic evil in alcoholic beverages. On this point an analogy might be drawn to automobile accidents in the 20th century; although reckless driving is generally regarded as a grave problem, cars are not held to be evil in themselves, and few seriously suggest eliminating them.

This attitude toward the use of alcohol was based on centuries of experience in England. Controls even in the days before Henry

VIII had been concerned with minimizing excessive drinking, especially among the clergy; with tariffs and regulation of imports; standardization of weights, measures, and quality; price; limitations on the number of taverns; closing hours; punishments for breach of the peace because of drinking, and the like. Licensing of taverns long antedated colonial times; and the idea that the business of dealing in alcoholic beverages was different from other businesses and existed only by special and revocable permission of governmental authority was well established by 1600. Long before this it had been clearly perceived by government agencies that control of trade in alcoholic beverages within the country as well as in foreign commerce could serve to bring in revenue.

Baird generalizes upon the precolonial development of the legal controls which were brought to this country:

"As with the laws against drunkenness and tippling, so it was with trade, taxing, and licensing legislation. None of these varieties came suddenly into being. And the purposes were often combined. It is sometimes difficult to determine whether a particular statute had to do with trade development for taxing purposes, or with licensing for price-fixing purposes, . . . for the control of drunkenness and other disorders, or for the sake of revenue alone. What is apparent is that there was a relationship between types, almost in the nature of cause and effect. In fact, there is reason to believe that the laws against drunkenness and tippling grew out of the weaknesses of the licensing laws; that licensing came about because the price-fixing program had run into difficulties; and that price fixing had itself been merely a logical extension of statutes which established uniform measures and coinage. That the business of control piled upon control had also demonstrated attractive opportunities for revenue to the state, was a discovery early appreciated and not long left unexploited."

With the changes in patterns of consumption which took place in the 18th and early 19th centuries—the great increase in the use of distilled spirits, and the development of frontier drinking and its urban counterpart—a new conception of the problems of drinking arose, and a new program to meet those problems. Although originating in England about 1750, the new movement soon appeared in this country and then in size and speed of growth, in scope and intensity, swept far beyond its English counterpart. This was the Temperance Movement, whose beliefs and activities have exerted very considerable pressure on American society for almost a century and a half. The movement originated in complaints about and proposals to control the behavior associated with excessive drinking. It differed from earlier attacks on drunkenness in two significant ways: it was organized, and it was concerned specifically with distilled spirits. It opposed the use of this type of beverage for almost all but medical purposes and proposed that everyone renounce almost all other use; further, it opposed the buying and selling of spirituous liquors. It incorporated as well the criticisms of drunkenness on moral, medical, economic, and nationalistic grounds common to earlier programs of control. The first important enunciation of the new concept was made by John Wesley in 1753.

The American Methodists in general accepted this "Discipline," although during the 1780's and 90's Bishop Asbury felt that his clergy, while better than their flocks, indulged in far too much drinking. The Quakers, firm believers in moderation in all things, had repeatedly warned against excess in drinking since the early 1700's, and by the end of the century had adopted a position similar to the Methodists'. By 1789 the belief that the use of distilled spirits was bad and that something should be done about it was widely held. In Connecticut a group of prominent citizens pledged themselves to carry on their business affairs without the use of distilled spirits and to serve their employees nothing stronger than beer and cider. When the first Congress was asked to place a prohibitive tariff on imports of spirits, it was argued by some that a moral issue was involved, one greater than support of domestic industry or increased government revenue. Many physicians, following the lead of the famous Dr. Benjamin Rush, stated that the use of distilled spirits was wholly unnecessary since they neither increased working efficiency, as had been generally believed, nor served any useful purpose as a medicine. Few of the temperance proponents, whether businessmen, farmers, physicians, or clergy, were relying on legislative means to gain the desired end. Moral suasion and personal example were their principal methods.

The new movement spread rapidly; before 1820 local societies to suppress intemperance were to be found in all the New England states, New York, and Pennsylvania. By 1827 a national organization existed with 216 local societies. The total population of the United States in 1830 was less than 13,000,000, but in 1833 there were 500,000 members in nearly 4,000 local temperance societies. During the next three years women were allowed to become associate members and children's groups were established, chiefly in Sunday schools.

McCarthy and Douglass comment on the close of the first phase of this historical development:

"The temperance movement in the United States reached a peak in 1836. Its work was publicized through eleven weekly and monthly journals devoted solely to temperance, and in the columns of many religious journals which were eager to open their pages to temperance writers. These publications were significant because they could disseminate information in popular language to the people. They were especially effective in ridiculing the idea that spirits prevented disease or that alcoholic beverages were of benefit to man. The journals featured statements by physicians and published a number of scientific articles.

"Many groups in the population were receptive to the temperance teachings. There was, for example, a Congressional Temperance Society in Washington, composed of members who were abstainers. There were temperance societies in a number of state legislatures. Their purpose was not to lobby for legislation but rather to exemplify the ideal of temperance by their conduct. Farmers and employers in industry were becoming convinced that cold water was a satisfactory beverage for working men. Temperance hotels were springing up in various cities. Massachusetts temperance leaders boasted that every town had at least one hotel in which spirits were not offered for sale. Temperance activity in the colleges received considerable publicity. In 1834 Horace Mann, who was to become a leader in the free education movement, advocated a young men's temperance society in every town. Apparently this wave of enthusiasm commanded more than lip service: distilleries were closing everywhere.

"It appeared to the optimistic leaders of the temperance forces that victory was within their grasp. To over a million members who were active in the movement it appeared reasonable to assume that moral suasion would bear fruit. Enthusiasm ran high in county and state conventions and a number of leaders predicted that within a few years an intoxicated person on the street would be a rarity."

The year 1840 can be noted as a turning point in both drinking customs and reaction to them. Up to this point the Temperance Movement had been logically directed against drunkenness, and against the use of distilled spirits, which dominated the consumption of that time. From this point on, developments were not so consistent. While the use of hard liquor declined relatively, and while both frontier drinking and drinking in commercial places showed relative decreases in importance, the philosophies and activities of temperance groups became increasingly radical, militant, and restrictive.

Between 1836 and 1840 the philosophy of the Temperance Movement shifted from opposition to the more than occasional use of distilled spirits to opposition to the use of any alcoholic beverage at any time; the new goal was total abstinence. This change to a radical position occurred with the growing but far from universal acceptance of two theories about alcohol. One, which has already been discussed, differed from the view of Wesley, holding that alcoholic beverages have no virtues whatsoever. This view was reinforced by medical men who agreed with Rush and by many farmers and businessmen who publicly rejected the belief that alcohol supplies working energy. The second theory was based on a new interpretation of Christian belief about alcoholic beverages. Up until 1840 the prevailing religious belief was that all Christians should abhor drunkenness and other excess related to drinking, but that alcoholic beverages were not evil in themselves since they were created by God and were clearly approved in both the Old and New Testaments. The new and radical belief was that the use of alcoholic beverages was not sanctioned by God and that wherever the Bible referred to wine in terms of disapproval it meant the

fermented juice of the grape while statements approving wine always referred to the unfermented variety. Neither theory was accepted by all the early temperance leaders, and dissension on the
newly proposed religious doctrine has been sharp and continuing.
The new theories reduced both the total numbers of members and
of organized temperance groups; they also made it impossible for
the churches to take a united stand in the new and radically
oriented temperance movements.

At this same time a second major change in temperance philosophy occurred. Prior to 1840 temperance was to be achieved by
persuading individuals voluntarily to limit their use of alcoholic
beverages. Now that total abstinence was the goal, the proposed
means of achievement became legal enforcement. State legislatures
were constantly petitioned for increasing controls on manufacture
and sale, with the ultimate goal of total prohibition to be enforced
by governmental sanction. This radical change also created dissension within the movement, a minority holding that to substitute
the constable for the teacher and preacher was an admission of
defeat, that persuasion, not coercion, was the only effective means
to reform morals and manners.

Changes in the nature of the personnel and leadership of the
movement also began to appear around 1840. The early temperance groups were composed of men only, and were spearheaded
by leaders from the professions and business. Their interests extended beyond securing pledges of temperance or renunciation
of the use of distilled spirits; they were social groups as well, and
active in mutual aid and community improvement. During the
1830's these men's groups began to extend membership to women,
who eventually became equal if not dominant participants in the
movement. Another new source of impetus was reformed drunkards who during this period were often the most forceful advocates
of eliminating the liquor traffic and signing pledges of total abstinence. The Temperance Movement, especially in its dramatic
manifestations, came more and more to be associated with programs of women's rights, above all suffrage and higher education.
Activities included street demonstrations by women which sometimes led to destruction of tavern property, and inflamed emotional
appeals by individuals whose background and lack of emotional

stability were hardly calculated to breed confidence among the business and professional men who had once lent leadership to the temperance cause.

Outside as well as inside the increasingly militant Temperance Movement the belief that "something had to be done" continued to grow, with the rise of a large body of opinion that disagreed with the philosophy and tactics of the temperance campaigners yet deplored excesses of drinking. In the South a special factor tended to increase anxiety, no matter what the attitude toward organized temperance groups. This was the use of alcohol by Negroes. It is necessarily frightening to members of the dominant group in a caste system when the casting off of controls that alcohol facilitates takes place among members of a suppressed group. Emancipation and the unsettled conditions following the Civil War markedly increased these fears, adding strength to the forces calling for ever stricter limitations on the sale of alcohol.

Another reason for concern about drinking was the enormous increase in mechanization in American society, with the resultant need in a wide variety of activities for a degree of precision, regularity, uniformity, and responsibility never before required. This change, which was made dramatically apparent, after 1920, in automobile driving, was perhaps felt first and most widely in industry. Mechanization, with its accompanying costly investments in machinery and its needs for specialization, interdependence, and teamwork, made industry increasingly sensitive to carelessness, personal aggression, tardiness, and absence—all characteristics of the heavy or excessive drinker.

One result of the increasing concern about drinking and its problems felt by groups with conflicting views both as to the nature of the problem and also as to means of control was vacillation and confusion in the programs of action which were adopted. Each of the three waves of governmental prohibition during the last 100 years has been followed by retraction of the prohibiting legislation. In the early 1850's state prohibition of the manufacture, distribution, and sale of alcoholic beverages became effective in all the New England states and in Minnesota, Michigan, Indiana, Delaware, Iowa, Nebraska, and New York—more than a third of the 31 states then in the union. By 1863, 8 of these 13 states had repealed and 4 others significantly modified this legislation.

The second wave occurred in the 1880's and involved eight states. Again the experiment was short lived, most of the states repealing the legislation by 1904.

Soon afterward the third wave appeared; by 1917 25 states had prohibitory legislation and two years later national Prohibition, more stringent than much of the state legislation, was achieved. In 1933 that too was repealed.

Much has been made of the hypocrisy of "drinking Wet but voting Dry," which was not uncommon in this 100-year period— although its incidence has perhaps been exaggerated. In some instances very real hypocrisy may have been present, but by and large most of this behavior can be considered hypocritical only from the narrow view adopted by militant Wets and Drys. Both groups have labeled "Dry" anyone who has voted for or otherwise supported controls. But many who have not accepted the philosophy or tactics of the Temperance Movement have voted for a Dry legislative program only because no other program of control was available.

The fluctuations in political action and the allegations of hypocrisy are but reflections of a far more significant confusion in moral and intellectual attitude. The questions associated with excessive drinking have been related to almost every important problem area in American life. Often drink has been represented as the cause of a variety of other problems. Many people, perhaps the majority, have reacted to the dominance of the radical total abstinence movement —its aggressive leadership in organizing and propagandizing—with moral timidity, confusion, escapism, and occasional outbursts of ineffective anger. Lack of any effective unified leadership outside the temperance groups largely accounts for the vacillation exhibited by the American people in regard to alcoholic beverages.

A great variety of legislation has been passed to control all aspects of production, distribution, and sale of beverages. Undoubtedly no other business has been so surrounded by legal restrictions. These laws vary among the different states and from legislative session to session within states. They concern zoning, sanitation, whether patrons shall stand up or sit down, labeling, advertising, shipping, service of food with drinks, permits for purchasers, all the controls mentioned for earlier centuries, and a multitude of other statutes, ordinances, and administrative rulings. Enforcement is extraordinarily diffuse in nature, sometimes lodged in special state boards, sometimes in local police departments, and invariably participated in by health, revenue, safety, and other administrative branches.

As government pressures became greater, the businesses concerned—whether restaurants, brewers, bottlers, distillers, vintners, or others—have showed tendencies to organize to resist prohibitory and profit-reducing actions of government and the many attacks of the temperance advocates. These attempts at organization never achieved the coherence, continuity, or emotional strength of the Dry movement, partly because of the economic competition between those concerned but more profoundly for lack of any positive moral program.

The impact of the temperance forces upon government was probably most effective, at least in a tactical sense, in the field of public school education. Legislation was passed in every state requiring education about alcohol. There was no question as to the nature of this education: it followed the line of the militant temperance program.

At the present time American drinking practices and attitudes—and the philosophies and programs for meeting the problems associated with drinking—can still be summed up in the one word: confusion. Drinking practices themselves have been undergoing marked change for a century. However, social responses to them have continued to be based largely upon philosophies stemming from practices and problems common to the period 1700 to 1840. Some religious and educational institutions, after a period of fairly united adherence to the radical temperance program, have shown a tendency since 1930 to withdraw from that position, without, however, adopting any other positive stand. There has seemed to be no room for any stand, philosophic, ethical, political, or otherwise, between the rigid extreme position of the Temperance Movement and the rather undefined position of its opponents, which has been centered in the liquor industry and is more a denial of the temperance position than a positive program in its own right.

This lack of behavioral and moral unity or integration has been clearly reflected in the action programs for dealing with the immediate, never-ending problems of drunkenness, accidents resulting from drinking, and alcoholism. Leaders in scientific research, medicine, rehabilitation, education, and religion (other than the radical temperance advocates) all remained aloof or retreated from the controversy. Such potential sources of leadership as foundations, universities, the medical profession, social and welfare agencies, industry, the military, the law, have for the most part failed even to admit they recognize the problems. When some action has been demanded by the public in the face of repeated dramatic and painful incidents, as in the case of the Skid Row population, the matter has been left by default to the jails and to mission groups.

The absence of accepted leadership has been reflected above all in the lack of knowledge about drinking, in the distaste for recognizing problems, and in the failure to present youth with an effective structure of beliefs, compatible with custom, on which consistent, realistic, and confident behavior and attitudes can be based. For the majority of Americans at this mid-point in the century there is still a great deal of inconsistency, unreality, and both moral and intellectual uncertainty connected with drinking. The problems related to it are far-reaching, painful, and costly. The responses to them are ineffective, highly variable, and accompanied by frustration and conflict. Some part of the social confusion is explained by the historical background. But effective understanding cannot be achieved until the basic facts about drinking behavior are available.

This uncertainty and confusion with respect to the drinking customs of the larger society has been reflected quite naturally in the particular area with which this book is concerned—drinking in college. Before presenting our survey findings, we shall discuss some specific examples of common reactions to the subject of drinking in college.

CHAPTER 3. *Common Reactions*

to College Drinking

Broad generalizations are often made about specific types of behavior or kinds of people on the basis of prominent characteristics exhibited only by certain members of the group. Thus college professors are described as absent-minded, and women as poor drivers. The fact that the majority in these groups do not display the behavior in question tends to be overlooked. Popular stereotypes of this kind are continually reinforced by isolated episodes of a humorous or dramatic nature and are thus perpetuated in folklore. Behind each of these beliefs can be found convincing but faulty reasoning.

These stereotypes may become so firmly established in popular belief that they are unthinkingly accepted even by persons intimately acquainted with individuals who do not fit the picture. One may know ten professors, of whom only one is occasionally forgetful, and still think of professors as absent-minded; or ten women drivers, not one of whom is incompetent, and still subscribe to the idea that women drive badly.

Misconceptions of this kind which relate to a social problem can seriously impede effective understanding of the problem. In turn, if realistic appraisal of a problem is lacking, attempts to alleviate or prevent it will not be aimed at the real source of the difficulty. We have just seen that this condition is illustrated in the history of attempts to deal with alcohol in the United States; it is also a factor of considerable significance with respect to drinking by college students. In this chapter a number of common reactions to the subject of college drinking will be considered. These include 1) the belief that student drinking is widespread, frequent, and excessive, 2) the idea that it is a subject for humor and satire, 3) a tendency to assume that unfortunate incidents which are associated with student drinking are all caused by the drinking, and 4) a feeling that facts about the matter are potentially dangerous.

A review of some of the innumerable references to college drinking in newspapers and magazines indicates that it is usually assumed that many students drink, that most of these drink frequently and to excess, and that the result is usually intoxication, often leading to situations involving serious problems, embarrassment, or disgrace. Publicity about undesirable incidents involving students often takes it for granted that drinking was an underlying factor. A recent news item about vandalism which occurred during a college outing reported in one paragraph that it had been positively traced by local police to a group of town troublemakers, yet in the next paragraph quoted a dean at the college as assuming that his students were responsible and placing blame on the "liquor problem." As in the case of the absent-minded professor or the poor woman driver, people tend to be impressed by every unfortunate incident involving students and drinking and to overlook the fact that most student drinking has no untoward consequences. We can illustrate from our own experience with this study how college drinking stereotypes are perpetuated by humorous treatment or association with dramatic incidents. And this is accompanied by a reluctance to seek facts apparently based on a fear of reality and its implications.

Drinking was fairly common in the oldest American colleges from the time of their founding. In the 18th century there were student canteens called "butteries" where all sorts of supplies including wines, beers, and liquors were sold. A regulation passed at Harvard in 1734 stipulated that no resident in the college should make use of distilled spirits or mixed drinks such as punch or flip in entertaining other students or strangers, and that no undergraduate should "keep by him brandy, rum or other distilled spirituous liquors." The intention was to supplant strong beverages with beer and wine, which were not only sold in the butteries but also served in college dining halls.[1]

In a review of student drinking and of trends in college policy toward it, Harry S. Warner, a temperance educator long interested in the subject, depicts vacillation and conflict in areas of control and behavior which reflect in great measure the changes that have been described in Chapter 2 for society at large. Warner concludes: "College alcoholic pleasures, customs, and consequences are not different from those elsewhere in influential society. They are a cross-section, a spectacular exhibit of the rapidly moving life and thought of the day. Notwithstanding age-old traditions peculiar to colleges, honored and retained here and there, and the outbreaks of enthusiasm moistened with alcohol after big games, at fraternity, alumni, and other group affairs, liquor enjoyment is not 'collegiate.' Resort to it and dependence upon it follow social, class, family, and community standards. But as a feature in publicity and public interest student drinking has a clear place of its own." [2]

The headlines and columns of the daily press furnish ample evidence to support Warner's statement that student drinking is prominent in the public interest. The findings of our own study certainly substantiate his conviction that student drinking is not primarily a product of the college experience. And yet a common stereotype continues to hold the colleges responsible.

The death of two students which occurred during drinking parties in 1949, and a third incident that year in which a student almost died while being initiated into a drinking club, stirred sharp condemnation of college administrators. Under the headline "Drinking Blame Put on College Rulers," the *New York Times* [3] quoted the head of an intercollegiate fraternal organization as condemning irresolute college administrators for condoning much of the excessive drinking and moral laxity revealed on college campuses.

Illustrations of popular reactions to the subject of college drink-

1. "College Drinking Customs," *Standard Encyclopedia of the Alcohol Problem*, 2 (Westerville, Ohio, 1924), 646–652.

2. *Alcohol Trends in College Life* (The Board of Temperance, Prohibition, and Public Morals of the Methodist Episcopal Church, 1938; pamphlet), p. 41.

3. March 20, 1949.

ing are legion. Because of their striking pertinence to this study we will review them by considering various responses to publicity about our own survey. March 1949, a few months after actual survey operations had commenced, seemed like an appropriate time to issue a press release announcing the survey and explaining its procedures and purposes. The decision was prompted by the numbers of inquiries that had been received from reporters, writers, and others who had heard about the study from the students. Great care was taken in the release to avoid giving any occasion for humor, sarcasm, or sensationalism. The release as prepared by the Yale University News Bureau read in part:

"A survey of the drinking habits and attitudes of college students around the nation is being conducted at Yale University . . . by the Section on Alcohol Studies of the Laboratory of Applied Physiology.

"This . . . survey is concerned solely with determining the nature, incidence and development of drinking behavior and its relationship to other aspects of behavior.

"There are no facts available on the drinking habits and attitudes of our college population. . . . Instead, there is a large mass of subjective opinion and misinformation on the subject. As a result, many sincere persons have acquired a distorted impression of the nature of the drinking behavior and problems in the American college.

"The survey directors say that their work should help educators in evaluating the need for and the development of alcohol education programs, should assist administrators and other persons charged with discipline, and should provide a broader base for understanding of student behavior among those affected by student activities, graduates, parents and college town residents.

"In addition, . . . the study should prove useful for college mental-hygiene and health authorities in working with psychological or medical problems in which drinking is a concomitant factor. . . ."

This release was used as the basis for rewritten stories issued by three national news services which appeared in hundreds of papers. And several editorial writers and columnists also discussed the survey.

The release was issued in the hope that a clear statement would prevent the spread of distorted reports about the study. This purpose boomeranged. The various ways in which the press handled the story provide excellent illustrations of college drinking stereotypes.

The Associated Press ran it as follows:

"How much do college students drink and why? Is drinking as fashionable on the campus as it was reputed to be in prohibition days when a flask on the hip was popularly supposed to be as necessary to the well dressed college man as a coon skin coat? The answers to these and other questions concerning the tippling habits of undergraduates are being sought by Yale research workers, the university announced today. . . . Co-directors of the survey say there's still a lot of talking about campus drinking but very few facts. The information they dig up they hope will be useful to college administrators, parents and health authorities. . . ."

Note that the main emphasis here, a comparison of present drinking with the fashionable flask-on-hip practices of prohibition days, was not mentioned in the original release. The word "tippling," a humorous word which connotes frequent if small drinks, was not ours. And that word set the keynote for such headlines as SEEK INFORMATION ON TIPPLING HABITS OF STUDENTS | YALE RESEARCH WORKERS GATHER DATA ON TIPPLING | COLLEGE TIPPLING TO BE SURVEYED | COLLEGE TIPPLING | COLLEGE STUDENTS' TIPPLING HABITS TO BE SURVEYED | COLLEGE TIPPLING DATA SOUGHT | PROBE TIPPLING HABITS OF COLLEGE STUDENTS | CAMPUS TIPPLING SURVEY IS PLANNED | CAMPUS TIPPLING PROBED | YALE UNIT TO PROBE COLLEGIATE TIPPLING.   Other headlines for the same story took the humorous approach, with frequent stress on how much students drink: LOTS, BECAUSE THEY LIKE IT. YES, BUT MORE SO | STEIN SONG QUIZ. | CHECK CAMPUS LIQUOR FACTS | HOW MUCH DO COLLEGE STUDENTS DRINK?

The International News Service story dealt primarily with well known college drinking songs: "There are plenty of college drinking songs, but Yale University wants to know: How many actually 'drink a high-ball at night-fall for Penn-syl-van-i-a.' Or 'Fill a stein for dear old Maine'; Or quaff a brew for 'C-o-l-u-m-b-i-a, Col-um-bi-ah!' and why? The Yale Laboratory of Applied Physiology has sent questionnaires to colleges in an effort to determine 'the nature, incidence and development of drinking behavior' among students.

. . . Meanwhile, Yale will get its facts about student drinking 'At a table down at Mory's.' "

As might be expected, the notes struck were echoed in most of the headlines: DRINKING SONGS THEME OF LATEST COLLEGE SURVEY | YALE ASKS HOW LITERAL ARE COLLEGE DRINKING SONGS | TODAY'S MYSTERY | SONGS TO SPARE, BUT HOW'S ABOUT SIP SUSCEPTIBLES? | HOW MANY "LIFT STEIN?" YALE WONDERS | "AT A TABLE—" COLLEGE DRINKING IS SUBJECT OF LATEST SURVEY | STEIN SONG YALE CHECKING ON COLLEGE DRINKING | AND NOW A SURVEY ON STUDENT TOASTS | YALE ASKS HOW MANY HIT BOTTLE? | YALE IS OUT TO FIND IF STUDENTS REALLY DRINK, DRINK, DRINK | DRINKING SONGS UNDER PROBE | WELL, PROFESSOR, MAYBE THEY MERELY HATE TO BE THIRSTY | ARE THERE REALLY YALE "WHIFFENPOOFS" | THERE ARE PLENTY OF COLLEGE DRINKING YELLS BUT YALE ASKS— | YALE LABORATORY SURVEYS COLLEGE DRINKING HABITS | YALE TO PROBE U.S. COLLEGES' DRINKING.

The United Press issued a somewhat longer story which included several direct quotations from our own release but again introduced new themes with stress on extensive drinking and humor:

"Yale University researchers today asked college students in a scientifically prepared questionnaire to let their hair down and tell all about their drinking habits and attitudes. The researchers started to poll students . . . to find out why they drink, and if they don't why not. The alcohol studies division of the Yale Laboratory of Applied Physiology . . . also wants to get the opinions of students on whether girls should take a cocktail now and then . . . to set the public straight on drinking in American colleges. Too many wild tales about guzzling students, they complained . . . The researchers want general background information and details about the student's college life. Other questions deal with what his parents think about fraternity beer parties and house parties where alcohol flows freely. . . . Abstainers will be grilled to find out just why they turn the stuff down. Ex-servicemen who return to the campus seasoned drinkers will be quizzed on their guzzling habits. They will be asked to explain about their elbow bending in the service and what effect returning to civilian life had on their drinking habits."

Headlines followed suit: YALE QUERIES UNDERGRADS ON ELBOW-

BENDING HABITS | YALE STUDIES LIQUOR HABITS | YALE GROUP
QUIZZES COLLEGE STUDENTS ON LIQUOR HABITS | TEACHERS QUIZ STU-
DENTS ON DRINKING HABITS | COLLEGE STUDENTS POLLED ON GUZZLING
HABITS | COLLEGE STUDENTS ASKED TO BARE DRINKING HABITS | SHOULD
GIRLS TAKE COCKTAILS NOW AND THEN? | YALE ASKING STUDENTS IN
COLLEGES WHY THEY DRINK OR NOT.

Two editorials about the study associated it with a recent trag-
edy: "It is something of a coincidence that this announcement
comes directly after . . . a student died after an attack by another
student who had been imbibing freely of intoxicants." [4] And "Announcement by Yale of a survey to be conducted of the drinking
habits and attitudes of students . . . on the same day as news
came . . . of the death of a junior after a fight which climaxed
a drinking party, is doubtless a coincidence. Many citizens, however, will regard this incident, which attracted public attention in
a particularly dramatic way, as a timely beginning of the study." [5]

Quite a different reaction came from a nationally syndicated
columnist who, after referring to the survey as a "Booze Kinsey,"
added:

"I can save Yale's section on alcohol studies of the University
Laboratory of Applied Physiology at New Haven a lot of time and
trouble. And heaven knows how much wear and tear on the tabulat-
ing machines. I can tell you now why college boys drink. They
drink because it is fun. Or else they think it's fun. Or else they
drink because the other guys do. Or else they do it because the prexy
says they shouldn't. But in any case it is my scientific observation
that nobody ever got hurt much by college drinking—unless he
was the sort of guy who would have been a drunk in college or out,
before or after.

"A college student is a puppy. He will chew any shoe, hat or soap-
bar that is placed before him. If he is a smart puppy he will stop
chewing the articles which make him sick. If he is a dumb puppy
he will keep on munching, and nobody can ride sufficient herd on
him to stop him.

"Yale, for some odd reason (maybe they haven't got enough work
to do in New Haven) would like to amass a flock of statistics. The

4. *Vermont Free Press,* Burlington, April 6, 1949.
5. *New Haven Journal Courier,* March 25, 1949.

snoopers would like to know if rich kids drink more than poor kids, or if the sons of teetotallers lush it up more than the scions of soaks.

"Every so often I despair of the work that satan finds for idle professional hands to do . . .

"The college boy or girl is one animal I should like to see protected from too much second guess and explanation. College is a fine, prime, giddy period of coltishness, where the hobblehoys cavort according to their nature. Their youthful troubles and their method of handling same swiftly serve as groundwork for the tough chores of adulthood, and as swiftly split the men from the boys . . .

"After this survey is finished, I have a suggestion for the surveyors: They might spend a few happy months investigating and correlating the motivation behind the startling phenomenon that babies invariably put everything they can reach into their mouths."

The columnist was not alone in expressing doubt about the study and its possible consequences. Ironically enough some people who voiced deep concern over the drinking habits of college students at the same time were fearful of factual information on the subject.

While the survey was in progress the head of a church-sponsored temperance organization wrote that although he thought much good could come from our "courageous experiment" members of his board shared with him the fear that "great harm to the cause of abstinence may also ensue." Serious concern about the study's possible findings was also expressed by at least one important representative of the liquor industry.

Several philanthropic foundations indicated that as a matter of course they avoided making grants for studies of drinking. One wrote: "In fact, this is a general field in which, as a policy matter, we have already given negative answers to requests." The president of another, in reporting that it would not be possible for his group to offer assistance, explained it as "entirely due to current commitments," and then added, "and in part to general policies."

Some college administrators were concerned over the consequences of the study. Only four colleges which were approached refused to participate,[6] but their reasons are significant. The dean of one declined because he feared the survey might lead to undesirable publicity and because it was "not clear how the results of such a survey could be used." Another college, where an unhappy incident involving drinking by students had recently received a good deal of publicity, merely reported that the administration "entertains grave reservations as to the wisdom of participating in your study." A dean who had originally initiated a request that his college be included later was forced to write: "It is with greatest regret that I tell you it seems inadvisable for us to cooperate in the study this spring. There is not complete sympathy with the project on the part of everyone who would be involved in the plans, and this is one reason for the negative decision. Another is that, in our judgment, this is not the psychological moment for us to project this study on our campus. I am more than sorry that we cannot be of service to you in this important work." The fourth turn-down came from a president who wrote: "We have a very strict rule here about drinking. It is a shipping [7] offense. Therefore it seems out of place for us to carry on such an investigation among our students. No one would want to incriminate himself." "Don't infer," he added, "that no drinking goes on." Many of the administrators who gave complete cooperation to the study requested that the participating colleges remain anonymous.

Still another common reaction to the study has been the assumption that the authors must be either for or against drinking. The Wet-Dry controversy has so dominated discussion and thinking about drinking in America that it seems inconceivable to many people that anyone would be interested in studying drinking customs from an objective viewpoint. Drinking biases are assumed to correspond with personal practice. It is implied that an abstainer would be against drinking, that a user would try to defend it. Questions about the authors' own drinking practices have been continual.

There are countless other illustrations of popular reactions and stereotyped beliefs about college drinking. Humor magazines pro-

6. Arrangements were not completed at several other schools merely because of conflicts in scheduling or the mechanical aspects of administration.

7. Automatic expulsion.

vide an abundance of one sort of stereotype, temperance literature another. Any book of popular college songs is rife with references to drink; it is not at all inappropriate that one of the stories about our own survey should have related it to song and verse.

Scanning the wide variety of evidence of their reactions, we find misinformation, anxiety, evasion, and frank expressions of fear of reality exhibited by educators, parents, reporters, and others concerned with the college scene. Clearly the confusion and lack of moral integration apparent for so long on the national level are reflected in reactions to drinking in college.

Against the background of stereotypes, conflicts, problems, and changing patterns of drinking and control that have been described, let us consider the facts about the drinking customs and attitudes of college students in the United States in the middle of the 20th century.

CHAPTER 4. *Who Drinks?*

Young people attending colleges in the United States are drawn from nearly every part of American society. Factors of race, religion, ethnic background, and social and economic class do not determine attendance at college or rule out the possibility of a college education. They undoubtedly influence the over-all probability of going to college, and are important in determining the particular type of college which a student will attend, for there are colleges to meet the needs of most social and cultural groups. The chief thing differentiating college students from the general population is age; the vast majority are between 17 and 23.

Because they have such diverse backgrounds and represent so many different social groups, it is dangerous to generalize about the behavior of college students. Of the students who participated in the drinking survey, it happens that three-fourths (74%) reported having used alcoholic beverages [1] to some extent, while a quarter (26%) reported having always been total abstainers. But data such as these, taken by themselves, may be quite misleading. The 27 schools which were included in the study were chosen as representing various types of college, but although they furnish a broad coverage of students with different social and cultural backgrounds, these do not necessarily represent all of America's college youth. Had other colleges been chosen the percentage of users of alcohol might have been different. Furthermore, 74% is not the incidence

1. User, unless otherwise indicated, refers to all students who have used alcoholic beverages apart from 1) experimental, joking, or ceremonial use before age 11, and 2) purely incidental, isolated experience. Amounts, frequencies, and beverages consumed will be discussed in Chapters 7 and 8.

46

of drinking by students at any particular college; and it does not take into account observed differences between the sexes. There were twice as many abstainers among the women (39%) as among the men (20%) who took part in the survey.

Different Types of College

Actually there were wide ranges of difference between colleges. The male students who had at one time or another consumed alcoholic beverages ranged from a high of 98% to a low of 55% at different colleges. Female students showed an even greater range, from a high of 95% to a low of 20%.

Colleges have been grouped in several categories in Table 1 and the incidence of use for each type of college determined. These categories include 19 of the 27 participating colleges. "Private, coeducational, dry" refers to colleges controlled by religious denominations which are known to look with disfavor on the use of alcoholic beverages.

Table 1: Incidence of Drinking,
          by Type of College (in per cent)

	Users of Alcoholic Beverages	
	Men	Women
Private, men or women only, nonsect.	92	89
Private, coed., nonsect.	92	84
Private, coed., "dry"	65	39
Public, coed., general	83	74
Public, coed., teachers	79	44
Public, coed., southern Negro	81	40

Among the male students, users include 92% of those attending private colleges for men and private coeducational colleges, roughly four-fifths of those attending public colleges of all types, and only two-thirds of those at private colleges controlled by "dry" religious denominations. Only at the private, nonsectarian, noncoeducational schools does the proportion of female users approximate the male. At public teachers' colleges, public Negro colleges in the South, and private "dry" colleges the proportion of abstainers among women greatly exceeds that among men.

In the colleges where drinking is most prevalent, the incidence of drinking among women comes closest to approximating that for men. Where there is less drinking, the incidence for men and for women is most sharply differentiated. This suggests that where sanctions against drinking are strongest their effectiveness is much greater for women than for men. The nature and extent of sanctions with respect to drinking will be explored further in Chapter 5.

Family Income and Type of College

The difference in prevalence of drinking found for the types of college described above might easily lead one to think that the type of college determined the incidence of drinking. Simple correlations of this sort rarely explain drinking or other customs and have all too often led to faulty conclusions and even faultier courses of action. Factors lying behind the attendance at one or another category of college may be much more significant for an understanding of the rates of abstinence or drinking than the matter of attendance itself at a particular type of college.

A very significant characteristic is the financial status of the students. It might be expected that students at private colleges would tend to come from families of greater means than those at public colleges, where tuition charges and living costs are less. In Table 2 the distribution of students in each type of college is shown according to their family income. Two facts stand out immediately; the comparative wealth of students at private colleges for men or women only and the relatively limited financial means of students in the public colleges, especially those for Negroes.

Within each category, female students consistently report higher family incomes than males. Perhaps this is because the mores of American society attach greater importance to providing a higher education for sons than for daughters. Families of limited means, if faced with a choice between sending a son or a daughter to college, will usually send the son. Also greater opportunities are generally available to men than to women for working in order to help finance their own college education. In our own study the proportion of men who held part-time remunerative employment while attending college (37%) was more than double that of women (16%). So a girl's chances of going to college appear to

equal a boy's only if her family's income is comfortably high. The
probability of attending a public rather than a private college is
also related to family income.

Table 2: Students' Family Income,*
by Type of College (in per cent)

Type of College	Male Students by Family Income			
	Under $2,500	$2,500– $4,999	$5,000– $9,999	$10,000 and over
Pvt., men, nonsect.	4	13	26	57
Pvt., coed., nonsect.	13	38	30	19
Pvt., relig., coed., "dry"	18	36	30	16
Pub., nonsect., coed., gen'l.	21	41	27	11
Pub., nonsect., coed., teach.	39	41	16	4
Pub., coed., southern Negro	65	26	7	2

Type of College	Female Students by Family Income			
	Under $2,500	$2,500– $4,999	$5,000– $9,999	$10,000 and over
Pvt., women, nonsect.	3	8	32	57
Pvt., coed., nonsect.	11	24	32	33
Pvt., relig., coed., "dry"	12	27	38	23
Pub., nonsect., coed., gen'l.	13	32	36	19
Pub., nonsect., coed., teach.	33	43	17	7
Pub., coed., southern Negro	66	19	9	6

* As reported by students.

Family Income and Drinking

Economic factors are important in determining the nature of
many aspects of behavior. Just as a person's wealth affects his choice
of a house, the clothes he wears, the people he associates with, the
food he eats, and may determine the college to which he sends his
son or daughter, so it also influences his use of alcoholic beverages.

The data in Table 3 on the distribution of users and abstainers
among all students in this survey, according to family income, confirm this statement. Among those students whose family income is
$10,000 or more, 86% of the men and 79% of the women drink.
The incidence of use varies directly with income down to 66%
of the men and 30% of the women for those with family incomes
below $2,500.

There are many ways in which income and participation in the drinking custom seem to be related. These will be considered fully in connection with other aspects of drinking, such as types of

Table 3: Incidence of Drinking, by
Family Income (in per cent)

| | Users of Alcoholic Beverages | |
Family Income	Men	Women
Under $2,500	66	30
$2,500–$4,999	74	48
$5,000–$9,999	81	58
$10,000 and over	86	79

beverage consumed, quantities usually taken, frequency, experience of intoxication, and various attitudes toward drinking. For the present, it is enough to point out that a student is more likely to have consumed alcoholic beverages if his family income is high, more likely to be an abstainer if his (or particularly her) family income is relatively low. Family income can be construed as a basic influence in the differences shown between rates of drinking at various types of college.

Cultural Group Membership

Cultural group membership (as defined by such components as ethnic background, racial origin, and religion) is another basic factor influencing many of our activities. People tend to live near, associate with, and emulate members of their own cultural groups. Drinking practices frequently reflect the customs and standards of the cultural group.

College students have been classified in this survey according to several cultural group criteria; Negroes have been differentiated from whites; students of the Protestant, Catholic, Jewish, and Mormon religious faiths have been distinguished; and a number of distinct ethnic groups have been identified by selecting students who trace a particular nationality in both of their parents for at least three generations.

Religion

The incidence of drinking determined according to religion for students who identified themselves as Protestant, Catholic, Mor-

mon, or Jewish appears in Table 4. The differences are consistent
with the different sanctions on drinking. The Jews have no sanctions against moderate drinking; in fact, for most persons who

Table 4: Incidence of Drinking, by Religious Affiliation (in per cent)

Religious Affiliation	Users of Alcoholic Beverages	
	Men	Women
Jewish	94	94
Catholic	90	78
Protestant	77	60
Mormon	54	23

identify themselves as Jews certain forms of drinking have an important association with religious ritual. The Catholic Church,
while not discouraging drinking in adults, often fosters abstinence
by young people. The various Protestant denominations are divided
on this issue; some strongly oppose drinking while others tolerate
moderate use of alcoholic beverages. Mormons are noted for severe
prohibitions. Among the religious groups where negative sanctions prevail, there are many more female than male abstainers.
This suggests, as in the case of similar differences according to
type of college, that as pressures against drinking in a college group
are stronger they are more effective for women students than for
men.

Table 5 examines drinking as related to degree of participation

Table 5: Incidence of Drinking, by Religious Affiliation and Extent of Participation in Religious Activity (in per cent)

Religious Affiliation and Participation	Users of Alcoholic Beverages	
	Men	Women
JEWISH: At least weekly	100	83
Irregular or none	91	93
CATHOLIC: At least weekly	90	80
Irregular or none	87	75
PROTESTANT: At least weekly	50	43
Irregular or none	84	68
MORMON: At least weekly	21	6
Irregular or none	77	48

in each of the religious groups. For Catholic and Jewish students the ratio of users to nonusers shows little change. Actually, regular religious participants are somewhat more likely to drink than the irregular or nonparticipants among Jewish men and Catholics of both sexes. Among Protestants who attend church weekly (both men and women) abstainers equal or out-number drinkers, while drinkers prevail among the irregular or nonchurchgoers. Even more striking differences are found with Mormons; only one-fifth of the Mormon men who go to church regularly are users as compared with three-fourths of those who are less active in their religion. Only 6% of the more devout Mormon women drink compared with nearly half of the less active churchgoers.

From these data it should not be hastily concluded that religious sanctions, by themselves, are directly influencing the drinking practices of young people adhering to the particular faiths. It is possible that religious participation and incidence of drinking are both reflections of more basic factors with which they are associated in common.

Nationality

While religious orientation can usually be determined from the faith with which an individual identifies himself and the extent of his participation in the formalized functions of that religious group, factors of ethnic or nationality background are much more obscure and more difficult to isolate. This is particularly true in our heterogeneous American society.

Students were identified with a nationality group only if the dominant nationality could be traced to a common country of origin for both parents back to grandparents and the majority of great grandparents. Only students whose families had been in the United States for at least three generations were classified as Americans. These exacting criteria eliminated many with mixed nationality background from consideration. So that possible cultural differences could be identified, Negro students were considered separately, and students listing their religion as Jewish or Mormon were excluded from nationality group consideration. As seen in Table 6, among men the Russian students show the highest incidence of drinking, followed closely by French, Italians, Germans,

Scandinavians, Irish, British, American Negroes, and lastly by American whites. For women, those groups large enough for

*Table 6: Incidence of Drinking, by
Ethnic Group * (in per cent)*

	Users of Alcoholic Beverages	
Ethnic Group	Men	Women
Russian	92	—†
French	89	—†
Italian	88	—†
German	87	81
Scandinavian	86	—†
Irish	84	64
British	81	66
Negro	81	43
American	75	61

* Only those ethnic groups have been considered which contained at least 50 students.

† There were fewer than 50 women in these groups.

analysis show a similar rank order with the exception of the Negroes. The differential incidence of drinking between men and women is much greater for Negro college students than for any of the nationality groups considered, the rate for Negro men being twice that for women.

A further refinement of ethnic groups was made according to Catholic or Protestant religion, as shown in Table 7. Several of the ethnic groups were found to be predominantly Catholic or predominantly Protestant. Where the minority religious group was not represented by at least 50 students, only members of the dominant religion were considered. With one minor exception (Scandinavian Protestants ranked just above American Catholics) all Catholic groups contain higher percentages of users than do Protestant groups. Among the four ethnic groups which are represented in both religions, the British and German students show a higher incidence of drinking than Irish and American students within each religion. Ethnic-religious group findings are not shown for women since only four groups, all Protestant, were adequately represented.

A religious-nationality comparison was also possible for Mormon students of Scandinavian and British nationality backgrounds. Among both Mormon men and women the incidence of drinking

Table 7: Incidence of Drinking (Men Only), by Ethnic Group and Catholic or Protestant Religious Affiliation (in per cent)

	Users of Alcoholic Beverages
British, Catholic	92
Russian, Catholic	92
German, Catholic	91
French, Catholic	90
Italian, Catholic	87
Irish, Catholic	86
Scandinavian, Protestant	85
American, Catholic	84
British, Protestant	81
German, Protestant	80
Negro, Protestant	80
American, Protestant	73
Irish, Protestant	72

was less for those of British than for those of Scandinavian background. However, in all instances there was much less drinking among Mormons than among Protestants of comparable sex and nationality. A similar comparison between Jewish and other students of Russian and German nationalities shows a higher incidence of drinking among Jews for both men and women, regardless of nationality.

These cultural group comparisons indicate that both religious and nationality group memberships are apt to be influential factors in determining the probability that one will use alcohol. However, an examination of drinking according to these combined religious-nationality classifications clearly indicates that factors associated with religious affiliation are more basic than those associated with nationality. While significant nationality differences appear within each religious group, the religious influence is apparent regardless of nationality. Even the degree of difference in drinking rates between men and women is closely correlated with religious identification.

Student Drinking and College Life

Conspicuous drinking behavior on the part of students frequently draws condemnation on the college. It is assumed that student drinking is a problem centered in the college which can be blamed on undesirable college drinking traditions and inadequate discipline and control.

It is true that the incidence of drinking increases with each college year. Table 8 shows that for men there was an increase from 69% among freshmen to 87% among seniors. For women the in-

Table 8: Incidence of Drinking, by College Year (in per cent)

College Year	Users of Alcoholic Beverages	
	Men	Women
Freshman	69	46
Sophomore	81	59
Junior	83	66
Senior	87	77

crease was more marked, from 46% among freshmen to 77% among seniors. However, it must be remembered that these students are at a rather crucial age in relation to drinking. During their college careers most of them come into their legal majority. Each advancing year increases the probability that experimentation in the adult custom of drinking will be tried. It is possible that the increased incidence of drinking in each college year merely reflects an increased tendency to drink as a boy or girl grows older which could be observed for all young people regardless of attendance at college.

Furthermore, a majority of the college students who drink started doing so before entering college. As already stated, first drinking refers to drinking apart from experimental, joking, or ceremonial use before age 11. Four out of five of the men and two-thirds of the women who had ever used alcoholic beverages had their first drink before coming to college (Table 9).

Drinking by Parents

A further indication of the importance of precollege influences can be found in a comparison of student drinking with that of

Table 9: First Drink before or after Entering College (in per cent)

First Drink	Students Who Are Users	
	Men	Women
Before entering college	79	65
After entering college	21	35
Total	100	100

their parents. Among the men, more than 9 out of 10 who reported that both parents drink are themselves users, compared with only 58% of those reporting that both parents abstain (Table 10).

Table 10: Incidence of Drinking, by Drinking Practices of Parents (in per cent)

Parental Drinking	Users of Alcoholic Beverages		
	Men	Women	Men and Women
Both parents use	92	83	89
One parent uses	83	54	75
Both parents abstain	58	23	54

Among the women the relationship is even more marked. When both parents drink, 83% of the female students are drinkers, compared with a mere 23% when both parents abstain. These data suggest that parental example is a factor of major significance in drinking by young people. They reinforce previous suggestions that as negative sanctions increase they do so disproportionately for women. In Chapter 5 the relative influence of advice about drinking offered by parents will be considered, and in Chapter 6 we shall review some of the factors which are associated with incidence of drinking among parents.

It is certainly not surprising to find a tendency for students to follow the example of their parents in deciding whether or not to drink. Actually, in so doing they are also conforming with the customs of the social groups to which they belong. Normally,

drinking is a social custom, and the drinking practices of an individual are apt to reflect those not only of his family but of friends
and companions. Students who reported that the majority of their
close friends drink were for the most part drinkers themselves,
while those whose close friends mostly abstain were with little exception abstainers too (Table 11).

Table 11: Incidence of Drinking, by Drinking
Practice of Close Friends (in per cent)

Drinking by Close Friends	Users of Alcoholic Beverages	
	Men	*Women*
Close friends drink	89	79
Close friends abstain	16	5

Summary

We have said that the present survey "happened" to show 74%
of the students reporting having used alcoholic beverages to some
extent, and that such a figure taken by itself is likely to be misleading. It should not surprise any reader to find 74% quoted in
newspaper or magazine articles and on occasion referred to with
alarm. It is likely to be used with the implicit or explicit assumption that this proportion of students "drink." Both writers and
readers will feel free to interpret that word according to their
pleasure, a freedom that will, if past history is a guide, extend to
license.

The phrase "having used alcoholic beverages to some extent"
requires definition. For this we must refer the reader to Chapter
8, where the "extent" of drinking in terms of frequency and quantities of beverage consumed is examined in detail. Here we are concerned only with the incidence of at least some drinking as opposed to abstaining. It has been stressed that over-all numbers or
percentages measuring the incidence of drinking, no matter how
defined, cannot be very useful and may well be misleading. For
example, if one were to assume that 74% of the students at X
college were drinkers, a concrete study at that institution might
well show the assumption to be far from fact. The real figure might
be 30%—or 90%. However, an estimate of the percentage of drinkers based upon the type of criteria presented in this chapter would

be found upon test to be very near to actuality. The estimate of 40% drinkers for women in a southern Negro college or 90% for men in a private, nonsectarian, coeducational college would, under ordinary circumstances, be found correct within a few percentage points.

Being aware of such criteria can be very useful in immediate, practical situations. For example, the count of users and nonusers in a given college over a period of years might show a 10% increase in users. This fact could well bring forth objections and strong criticism from parents, alumni, faculty, administration, and local groups; it might also elicit new regulations, policies, and punishments which would be generally disturbing to the educational institution. But the increase might have resulted from a change in the sex or age ratio of the students, from a decrease in enrollment among certain Protestant sects or an increase in the proportion of students with families in the higher income brackets. The possibly frightening implications of the statement "10% increase in student drinkers in last six years" might be wholly false, the objections misplaced, and the consequent actions unnecessary.

It was a purpose of this chapter to underline the conception that the use of alcoholic beverages is a social phenomenon, a custom. Certainly the figures presented so far would suggest that drinking or abstaining is not a way of behavior which is selected by individuals operating as separate, willful entities unaffected by social environments. College men or women do not select their parents, their sex, or their ethnic affiliations; and few determine their religious affiliation or the income or drinking behavior of their parents. Yet even these few factors, especially when combined, may be seen to be of considerable importance in determining what behavior is likely to be adopted.

Understanding the social and cultural aspects of drinking behavior also has immediate practical uses. One of these is in the field of formal education. Have the materials and value judgments commonly used in American grade schools and the first two years of high school been developed with perception or understanding of these social forces? Is it not possible that some of these teachings, which state that alcohol is a poison, that drinking is evil, that drinkers are on the road to disease, death, crime, drunkenness, and the like, are so inconsistent with the experience and belief of portions of the student bodies that their educational effect is nonexistent or perhaps weakening to educational processes in general? At least such questions may be asked, once the nature of drinking as a custom is appreciated.

Finally, it should be reiterated that our data come from a portion of one segment of American society; they are not a representative sample of that society or of that segment. They may be representative samples of certain categories of those attending American colleges in the mid-20th century. There is evidence in this survey which indicates that the habits of many between the ages of 17 and 23 are different from the habits of 11 to 16. There is other evidence indicating that for most groups in the population drinking habits change with age.

Taking the data of this study to apply to all young people between 17 and 23 or to all adults is certainly not warranted. However, the questions which arise and the more general understanding which develops from this study could be exceptionally useful in application to wider areas. This is especially true because no systematic studies have ever been made of who drinks in our society.

The facts we have presented about who drinks might suggest that college campuses were inhabited by a race of robots: that if certain buttons were pushed (family income, religious affiliation, parental custom), the students would drink; if other buttons, they would be abstainers. Although it is probably true that most members of our society underestimate the influence of society and culture and markedly overestimate the function and range of rational, individual control, it is equally true that a picture of human beings as puppets of some societal machine is fallacious. Of the many reasons for rejecting such a fallacy, two or three are particularly relevant for understanding drinking behavior.

Human customs are rarely of a narrow specificity. Ordinarily there is a range of acceptable behavior for adjusting to a particular situation. There is no rigid formula in ordinary civilian life for greeting a person, for eating breakfast, or for driving a car. The exceptional rigidities of dress, salutation, and even mode of walking in certain institutional settings contrast with and allow a clearer recognition of the usual flexibility. These exacting prescriptions may be called rituals and can be seen dramatically in certain military, religious, and judicial activities. Some nonritual situations also call for extraordinarily fine discrimination and precision if a particular goal is to be achieved or immediate danger avoided. Thus, there may be rigid prescriptions for cutting diamonds, for team operations on a tight rope, or for loading TNT. In many of our acts, however, such close adherence to precisely elaborated custom is unnecessary and, perhaps more important, might be inefficient. There are ranges of acceptable behavior with sometimes a few, sometimes many, possible modes of response. Such variation and flexibility are denied to the machine.

A second marked difference between the robot and the human being is in the matter of motivation. Within the human being there is motivation, which may well be inconsistent with the prescribed pathways of behavior. Many customs have developed which are functional primarily for the long-range welfare of the group but which restrict and frustrate the individual: sharing and taking turns are obvious examples. The robot receiving inconsistent or conflicting commands or impulses would presumably grind to a halt. In contrast, human beings are continually subject to such internal conflict but rarely collapse.

The third difference concerns the receiving apparatus. A robot may respond to 100 different signals, perhaps according to frequency or intensity of sound, but the signals are absolute. Whether simple or complex, the No. 3 signal remains the No. 3 and No. 99 remains No. 99. Wires and relays can get out of order, of course. If they do, it is conceivable that No. 3 signal might regularly call forth No. 24 response or, more likely, that the machine would break down. But a human being presented with signal 3 can transmute or translate it to 7 or 19 or 96. And receiving it the next time he may accept it as 3. Another difference can be seen in the degree of acceptance. The human being may respond to a stimulus lightly or partially or after delay, or he may respond intensely, fully, and immediately. Again, the mechanical actor can be reached by only one means, say pushing a specific button or making a certain light appear; a great variety of stimuli can set the human being in action. Furthermore, the human being seems capable of receiving messages which the sender never had in mind, which, indeed, he may deny having sent. Writers of mystery and science fiction have often created plots in which robots crossed this gap toward human abilities, while prophets of gloom have suggested the opposite trend in stories about humans.

This chapter surveys the phenomena of drinking from the viewpoint of the individual whose behavior was being studied. As he or she remembered and interpreted the memory, what messages were received bearing upon the drinking of alcoholic beverages? Who gave advice, command, or suggestion? Were the messages consistent or inconsistent? Parents, teachers, ministers, athletic coaches, physicians, friends, and college authorities are the major sources considered. In addition to the opinions, warnings, or suggestions received from others, there is the matter of the individual's own explanation of why he behaves as he does.

The way information, advice, or orders are received and personal opinion is formulated may differ significantly according to the age of the individual. Certainly young people in the age group 17 to 23 are faced with many difficult problems and decisions. This is the time when the strength and extent of ties of dependence on the parental family are reduced and responsibilities of independent living and independent thinking are increasingly assumed. It is the crucial period of transition from adolescence into adulthood as it is conceived in our society. One of the many questions which young people face during this period is whether or not to drink alcoholic beverages.

For many, this is by no means an easy matter to decide. While there are specific drinking customs in some cultural groups in America which form an integral part of various social functions, the use of alcoholic beverages is also associated with many abuses and has created numerous problems for our society. So young people are faced with conflicting pressures, sanctions, and even conflicting motivations with respect to drinking.

Some of them may have grown up in homes where they have watched their parents drink but have themselves been forbidden to do so. Explanations have often been inconsistent and inadequate in the face of parental example. Others, with parental example and even parental approval for drinking, may have met with strong conflicting advice from church or school. Still others may have grown up in homes where abstinence is both practiced and urged but later find themselves associated with groups where drinking is expected and where the abstainer is subjected to ridicule or ostracism or at least made to feel different and uncomfortable.

Students in the survey were asked whether they had ever received "specific advice concerning the use of alcoholic beverages." More than 90% reported yes (men, 91%; women, 92%). Furthermore, nearly half indicated that this advice had been designed to make them abstainers (men, 47%; women, 45%). Less than a fourth of

the students who were Jewish or Catholic by religion reported having received specific advice to abstain, as compared with about half
the Protestants and more than three-fourths of the Mormons.

At first glance there seems to be no doubt but that advice to abstain is associated with effective negative sanctions as far as drinking
is concerned. Of the men who had received such advice, 30% were
abstainers as compared with only 18% of those who had not been
so advised (for women, 56% and 35% respectively).

However, for those advised to abstain, rather startling differences
were found in the incidence of drinking according to the source of
the advice. As shown in Table 12, where it came from family members, only 60% of the men drank, as compared with 82% of those

Table 12: Incidence of Drinking, by Source of Specific
Advice to Abstain (in per cent)

	Users of Alcoholic Beverages	
Source of Advice to Abstain	Men	Women
From parents	60	33
From church (not parents)	84	50
From teachers (not parents or church)	90	77
No advice to abstain	82	65

who reported that they had never been advised to abstain. But
of those whose advice came from the church (but not from parents)
84% were users; and of those advised to abstain by schoolteachers
(but not by parents or church) 90% drank. So it appears that
while sanctions against drinking are definitely effective (as compared with no negative sanctions) when they come from parents,
advice not to drink which originates with the church or school may
be actually less effective than no advice.

Among women somewhat similar findings occur. Only a third of
those whose families advised abstention were drinkers, as compared
with two-thirds of those receiving no such advice. However, half
the women advised against drinking by the church (and not by
parents) were drinkers, as were 77% of those advised by school
(and not church or family). As with the men, negative sanctions
originating in the family are associated with an impressively high
incidence of abstinence. Church sanctions appear more effective

than no advice, while sanctions coming from the school are actually associated with a greater incidence of drinking than no advice at all. A comparison of the four religious groups by incidence of drinking in relation to advice from the church to abstain shows no difference for Protestants, Jews, Mormons, and Catholics.

Reasons for Abstaining

While sanctions against drinking which originated in the church or with religious leaders do not appear to be directly associated with abstention by college youth, religious sanctions nevertheless appear to play a major role in the decision to abstain. All non-drinkers (including former drinkers) were provided with a check list of possible reasons for abstaining and asked to check a most important and a second most important reason. Factors of religion ("contrary to religious training," "immoral," or "pledged not to drink") were listed as most important by 34% of the male abstainers and as second most important by an additional 18%; as most important by 37% of the female abstainers and as second most important by an additional 20%. Thus, of the students who abstain, over half list factors of religion as major reasons for not drinking. In contrast just a third of the students listed disapproval by parents or friends as reasons for abstaining. These findings are not consistent with the relationship between incidence of drinking and the source of advice to abstain.

For purpose of comparison, reasons for abstaining have been ranked by a score which assigns a double value for listings as "most important" and a single value for listings as "second most important" reason. The large majority of these reasons are seen in Table 13 to fall into three groups: 1) dislike for the taste or ill effects of alcohol or a feeling that it is detrimental to health; 2) religious training, morality, or a pledge not to drink; 3) disapproval of family or friends. The concept of personal problem drinking does not assume great importance for young people who abstain. Very few abstain because they have lost control of their drinking in the past or because they cannot afford to drink. While a majority of the abstainers report that their close friends also abstain, practically none list that fact as a reason for doing so themselves. It is obvious that students' perceptions of their reasons for abstaining are not always consistent with certain measurable sanctions.

Comparatively few report that they abstain because of participation in sports. It is noted elsewhere (Chapter 9) that college athletes

Table 13: Value Rating * of Reasons for Abstaining, Based on Most Important and Second Most Important Reasons (in per cent)

Reasons for Abstaining	Students Who Abstain	
	Men	Women
Don't like taste, makes ill, or detrimental to general health	35	35
Contrary to religious training, immoral, or pledged not to drink	27	32
Parents or friends disapprove	12	16
Bad experience of someone else	7	4
Can't afford it	4	1
Interferes with participation in sports	4	1
Friends never use	1	2
Have lost control of drinking in the past	1	—†
Other	9	9
Total	100	100

* Based on the formula $\frac{2a + b}{\Sigma (2a + b)}$. a equals number of students who elected item as most important reason for abstaining; b equals number who checked item as second most important reason for abstaining.

† $<0.5\%$.

report a relatively high incidence of drinking when compared with students who do not take part in sports. On the other hand, participation in sports was the major reason cited by those students who report that they have at some time or other "gone on the wagon." Of those who did report going on the wagon (males only) and attributed this to some outside pressure, 47% listed participation in sports, 14% credited advice from parents, 15% the advice of a steady date, 9% the advice of a religious leader, 6% the advice of a doctor, 5% the advice of other friends, 4% cited school or college rules.

When reasons for abstaining are compared for students at different types of colleges, the only noteworthy difference which appears is that reasons of a religious and moral nature play a more prominent role for both men and women students from religious "dry" colleges than from other types of schools.

Comparisons according to religious affiliation reveal several notable differences. Reasons of religion or morality receive more than a 50% value rating from Mormons, as compared with about a 25% rating for Protestants, 15% for Catholics, and zero for the few Jewish abstainers. For Jewish students nearly all reasons cited are those of taste, ill effect and health. The "bad experience of someone else," which was rarely noted as important by Jewish, Mormon, or Protestant students, received ratings of 15 and 12% respectively from Catholic men and women.

No significant differences in reasons for abstention were found when abstainers were compared according to family income, although oddly enough "can't afford it" was given most frequently by students in the highest ($10,000 or more) family income brackets.

College Policy and Student Drinking

College students are not alone in facing difficult decisions about their drinking behavior. The problem has long bothered college administrators and continues to haunt them. The many letters of inquiry that have come from college officials in the course of preparing this study bear impressive witness to the deep concern and uncertainty of those responsible for molding college policy.

While giving questionnaires to students, members of the survey staff also discussed college policy toward student drinking with officials of most of the 27 colleges which participated in the study. They found no instance of a clear-cut policy with which deans and other administrative personnel were generally satisfied. Where there were stringent regulations forbidding drinking by students, administrators were aware of deep resentment and rather violent reaction on the part of some students. Where liberal policies were followed, administrators were sensitive to criticism from town residents and parents whenever incidents involving drinking by students occurred. As a result some college administrations have avoided formalizing any policy and have fitted regulations and official statements to the particular circumstances.

A measure of the uncertainty and vacillation in this area can be found in the students' own perception of the policy of their particular college. The question was asked: "In your opinion, what is the attitude of your college officials toward drinking on the part of students?" Space was provided for the students to formulate their own reply. Answers were classified, first independently and then jointly, by two members of the survey staff. Responses were grouped under "unqualified disapproval," "liberality or indifference," and several categories of conditional approval. Just over half of all the students (both men and women) felt that their college's attitude toward student drinking was one of unqualified disapproval, while 21% of the men and 15% of the women felt that college officials were liberal or indifferent to drinking. A complete classification appears in Table 14.

Table 14: *Students' Rating of Official College Attitude toward Student Drinking (in per cent)*

| | Students' Ratings | |
Classifications of College Attitude	Men	Women
Unqualified disapproval	52	54
Conditional (disapproval but tolerance)	7	10
Conditional (on amount and frequency)	16	16
Conditional (on age, place, behavior)	4	5
Liberality or indifference	21	15
Total	100	100

These responses represent the students' perception of an attitude or policy. Like all reports on attitude perception they are subjective interpretations of manifest actions. Although not specifically identified as sanctions, these perceptions define the college sanctions of drinking in the most meaningful way possible, not necessarily as they are perceived by those from whom they derive but as they are perceived by those toward whom they are directed. Let us now relate this perception to student drinking behavior.

First it is of interest to consider to what extent individual colleges have clear-cut attitudes, as perceived by their own students, toward drinking. That is, to what extent is there student agreement on the policy of their own school? Of the 27 colleges surveyed, there were 5 at which at least 75% of the students (men and women) perceived the college attitude as one of unconditional disapproval. At 3 the vast majority of students perceived either a liberal-indifferent or a conditional attitude (two of these were colleges for men only, the other for women only). At the other 19 schools substantial numbers of students assigned the college attitude to each of the extremes, indicating no general agreement as to the official attitude.

The students' perception of college policy is not likely to be objective. A college having what an objective observer would term a middle-of-the-road attitude might seem liberal to some abstainers because it tolerates drinking at all, yet disapproving to some heavy drinkers because it opposes heavy drinking. In a majority of the schools where the attitude was not clearly defined, it was found that abstainers were more likely to perceive a liberal attitude while students who were frequent users were more likely to perceive an attitude of disapproval.

It was also found that perception of an extreme attitude on the part of the college (either unqualified disapproval or liberality) was correlated with extreme personal views about drinking. Of the male students who in other questions expressed themselves either as positively disapproving or positively approving of drinking by others, 89% indicated a perception of extreme views on the part of college officials. On the other hand only 67% of those whose personal attitudes were conditional saw the college position as extreme.

To examine the relationship between perception of the college attitude toward drinking and actual student drinking behavior, colleges were ranked according to a liberality score determined by taking the percentage of student responses in each school which indicated a conditional attitude on the part of the college plus twice the percentage of responses which indicated liberality or indifference. When liberality scores are correlated with the per cent of users at each school it becomes clear that the more liberal the college attitude as perceived by the students, the more users in the college population.[1]

In a similar manner, the liberality score was correlated with the percentage of the users in each school who had ever reached the

1. Rank correlation coefficient (Spearman); for men N = 22, P = +.70; for women N = 17, P = +.64; both significant at the .01 level.

level of intoxication defined as "tight." [2] Findings here indicated no significant correlation, positive or negative.[3] Thus although college sanctions against drinking seem to be definitely associated with a lower incidence of drinkers at a particular school, they have no effect on the extent of drinking among users as measured by the criteria of having been tight. There is some suggestion, illustrated by a few selected schools, that, among male students, drinkers at "dry" schools are more apt to have been tight than those at schools with liberal sanctions.

A definite relationship appeared between the incidence of drinking or abstaining at particular schools and the extent to which male students who drink have experienced intoxication. The five schools having the lowest percentage of users ranked in the highest ten by percentage of users who have been tight. Exactly the same relationship was found at the next level of intoxication defined as drunk. There is certainly a suggestion here that male students who drink in violation of generally accepted practice are apt to go further in their drinking than students for whom the use of alcoholic beverages is more or less accepted behavior. This reaction is illustrated by the comment of a student in a southern "dry" college: "When you go to the trouble of driving 50 miles to drink, you don't have just two drinks."

In summary, it can be noted that the uncertainty and indecisiveness expressed by many college officials in personal conversations with members of the survey staff are reflected in the students' perception of college drinking attitudes and sanctions. While college sanctions may be correlated with the number of students who drink, they appear to have no effect on the extent of drinking among drinkers in any particular college.

Students' Explanations for Their Drinking

Having examined the various pressures and sanctions which students perceive being exerted to keep them from drinking, and hav-

2. The term "tight" is used in this study to describe a level of intoxication between "high" and "drunk." All three terms are defined and discussed in Chapter 10.

3. Rank correlation coefficient (Spearman); for men $N = 22$, $P = -.19$; for women $N = 17$, $P = +.12$.

ing reviewed the reasons for abstaining given by the nondrinkers, let us consider the explanations of the users for their drinking.

A check list of 13 reasons for drinking was provided.[4] Students were asked to indicate for each of the items listed whether it was of considerable importance, some importance, or no importance in his or her own use of alcoholic beverages. The items are listed in Table 15 in the order of importance assigned to them by male students.

It is not easy to explain why the reason "because of enjoyment of taste" leads the list of motivations for drinking as reported by both male and female students. Without imposing personal value judgments it can be said that we did not consider that most beverages containing alcohol were noted for a pleasing taste by a majority of drinkers. Different types of beverages have quite different tastes. If taste is such an important reason for drinking it might be expected that the ratings of taste would vary according to the particular types of beverage preferred or most frequently used. A comparison of importance ratings on taste was made according to the preferences for types of beverage reported by the students as well as according to the type of beverage most frequently used. It was found that ratings of the importance of taste as a reason for drinking showed no significant differences whether the type of beverage preferred or most frequently used was beer, wine, or distilled spirits.

Remembering that these motivation ratings represent merely the students' perceptions of the reasons why they drink, we offer as a possible explanation of the relative importance assigned to factors of taste the theory of the "rational man." The rational man seeks a sensible, logical explanation for all behavior and phenomena. The most logical explanations for ingesting foods and liquids are first that they are nutritious and beneficial to us and second that they have a pleasing taste. There being few arguments which hold alcoholic beverages nutritious or beneficial to the body, the factor of taste is the logical reason left for the rational man to use in explaining his drinking.

4. The determination of these particular reasons was made from the pretest responses to an open type of question on reasons for drinking.

*Table 15: Perception of Drinking Motivations. Relative Impor-
tance Attached to 13 Selected Reasons for Drinking (in per
cent)*

| Reason for Drinking | Degree of Importance for Men | | | | |
	Considerable	Some	(Total)	None	Total
Because of enjoyment of taste	29	43	(72)	28	100
To comply with custom	13	51	(64)	36	100
To be gay	16	46	(62)	38	100
To relieve fatigue or tension	13	41	(54)	46	100
To get high	12	35	(47)	53	100
To get along better on dates	4	30	(34)	66	100
As an aid in forgetting disappointments	5	21	(26)	74	100
In order not to be shy	4	21	(25)	75	100
To relieve illness or physical discomfort	3	22	(25)	75	100
For a sense of well-being	1	19	(20)	80	100
To get drunk	7	9	(16)	84	100
As an aid in meeting crises	1	8	(9)	91	100
To facilitate study	1	2	(3)	97	100

| Reason for Drinking | Degree of Importance for Women | | | | |
	Considerable	Some	(Total)	None	Total
Because of enjoyment of taste	22	47	(69)	31	100
To comply with custom	15	50	(65)	35	100
To be gay	8	44	(52)	48	100
To relieve fatigue or tension	7	36	(43)	57	100
To get high	3	14	(17)	83	100
To get along better on dates	4	35	(39)	61	100
As an aid in forgetting disappointments	2	10	(12)	88	100
In order not to be shy	3	15	(18)	82	100
To relieve illness or physical discomfort	6	26	(32)	68	100
For a sense of well-being	2	13	(15)	85	100
To get drunk	—*	1	(1)	99	100
As an aid in meeting crises	1	5	(6)	94	100
To facilitate study	—*	1	(1)	99	100

* <0.5%.

In a sense, all the reasons cited as of importance in drinking may reflect to some extent a groping for rational explanations. However, the reasons other than taste have a greater basis of reality in known physiological, psychological, or social functional value.

It is apparent in Table 15 that reasons having primarily a social connotation, e.g., "to comply with custom," "to be gay," "to get along better on dates," are generally considered of greater importance than those suggesting primarily a psychological motivation, e.g., "as an aid in meeting crises," "to get drunk," "for a sense of well-being," and "in order not to be shy."

There is a high degree of agreement between men and women in the relative importance which they assign to each reason for drinking.[5] In only two instances did the ratio of women ascribing importance to an item exceed that of men by even as much as 5%. Women to a greater extent than men think that they drink in order to get along better on dates and in order to relieve illness or physical discomfort. Both of these items deserve further comment.

At most of the colleges which participated in the survey, members of the survey staff were available for discussions with the students following the administration of the questionnaires. Students usually had a wide variety of questions: some dealing with physical or psychological reactions to alcohol; some with the questionnaire itself; some with problems of alcoholism, usually in reference to a particular alcoholic known to them; and some with personal confusion regarding their own drinking in the face of conflicting social pressures. College girls occasionally brought up the problem of feeling that they have to drink in order to be acceptable to their male dates. It is in this connection that we believe many of the girls have attached importance to the item "get along better on dates." That is, they drink because they feel it is expected of them in mixed company among certain social groups. They fear that if they don't drink they will not be invited again. This type of explanation is quite different from that referring to the relief from personal anxiety which alcohol may afford in boy-girl situations.

There is no doubt that alcohol, since it is a mild anesthetic, can

5. Based on an indication of some or considerable importance, Spearman's rank correlation coefficient between men and women is $+.91$, with an .01 level of significance.

provide genuine if temporary relief for certain types of physical discomfort. Its efficacy in physical illness is a matter on which physicians do not agree. Certainly it is prescribed in a medicinal sense less frequently today than formerly. To a considerable degree the use of alcoholic beverages for medicinal purposes is associated with survivalistic folk beliefs, and continues to be prescribed as a home remedy rather than by doctors' orders. There is one medicinal use for alcohol which is restricted to women—in connection with menstruation. Two questions on this use were included in questionnaire forms for women. Although about a third of the girls failed to answer one or both of these questions, approximately 7% of those who did reply reported using alcohol in connection with menstrual pain. In response to the other question 7% reported that alcohol has a greater appeal for them either just before, during, or just after the menstrual period than at other times. The girls who used alcohol for relief from menstrual pain were not necessarily the same ones who reported a heightening of alcohol appeal in connection with menstruation. This association of alcohol use with the menstrual cycle is sufficient to account for the sex difference in designating relief of illness or physical discomfort as a motivation for drinking.

The greatest discrepancy between the sexes was in items associated with the effect from drinking, such as "to get high," which was noted as of importance by 47% of the men and only 17% of the women, and "to get drunk," which was important for 16% of the men and for only 1% of the women. Only 12% of the women, as compared with 26% of the men, noted drinking "as an aid in forgetting disappointments."

A few interesting differences in perception of drinking motivations were noted among the religious groups. Jewish men and women ran ahead of all other religious groups in attaching importance to drinking to comply with custom. This was of some or considerable importance for more than 80% of the Jewish students, as compared with about 60% of the Protestants, Catholics, and Mormons. Catholic men ran considerably ahead of those of other faiths in ascribing importance to taste, as did Catholic women in the case of "relief of illness or physical discomfort." Mormon men, who when they drink do so mostly in the face of strong negative sanctions, attached greater importance than other men to drinking "to be gay," "as an aid in forgetting disappointments," "to get high," and "to get drunk." Mormon women put particular emphasis on "to be gay" and "in order not to be shy."

No significant differences in perception of drinking motivations were found among men or women of different family income levels.

Summary

Two approaches to a more effective understanding of drinking behavior have now been presented. The first indicated patterns of drinking or abstinence according to group membership or according to such characteristics as income of parents. The second concerned ideas or advice or commands given the individual by those in particular roles, and the individual's own explanation for his drinking or abstinence. Although the two approaches are quite distinct, both are essential for understanding the facts of drinking behavior. They are also interrelated: the types of advice received and of individual explanation both vary in accord with the category or group. The Jewish group, for example, showed few instances of commands to abstain and a greater tendency than those of other faiths to explain one's own drinking behavior on the basis of group custom.

The discrepancy between actual behavior and the message or norm presented by individuals or organizations attempting to initiate, maintain, or change behavior is of significance for teachers, ministers, parents, legislators, or others concerned with drinking or any other behavior. Often enough, perception of the discrepancy leads merely to condemnation of those not following the prescription, or to more intensive and extensive repetitions of command or advice. The two methods of approach just indicated permit of more effective response. They suggest that persons in different sociological categories present different degrees of susceptibility to techniques for changing, modifying, initiating, or blocking behavior. It is plain that advice for complete abstinence given uniformly to children of poor and wealthy parents, to southern Negroes and to Jews, to those of Mediterranean and English backgrounds, is going to be received variously and to be effective in extremely different degrees.

It is also clear that the agency or source of opinion or command is an important factor. A command issued by a father to his son may prove effective, whereas issued by a clergyman to the same boy it may have little effect. Social scientists are interested in developing generalizations about behavior, about the consistency or variability of various forms of behavior, and about the relative strength of different types of sanctioning agency for maintaining or changing behavior in a variety of situations by various techniques. The educator, minister, or parent wishes to make practical use of specific facts in particular situations. As patterns of behavior, rules, and opinions emerge from the data on student drinking, certain suggestions will be posed and more cogent questions will be asked aimed at providing new insights on both a theoretical and a practical level.

CHAPTER 6. *Drinking by Parents*

Our survey has shown that 89% of college students from homes in which both parents drink are drinkers and that 54% of those from homes where both parents abstain are abstainers. Clearly parental example is an important factor in the decisions of college youth about drinking. We have also seen that sanctions against drinking which originate with parents are more apt to have an effect on students' behavior than negative sanctions from other sources such as church or school. However, it should be noted that parental example was found to be far more significant than parental advice in influencing student behavior. Regardless of the advice factor, students are much more apt to abstain if both parents are abstainers than if one or both parents drink. Hence it is pertinent to consider the drinking practices of parents. We shall learn something in this way about a different generation in American society, men and women who are for the most part between 40 and 50 years of age, though limited to those whose sons and daughters are attending the colleges we surveyed and to the same additional factors of selection which define the student population studied.

It is important to remember that the information we have on the drinking practices of parents is indirect. It is actually the students' perception of their parents' behavior.

If we consider all of the fathers in our study together, we find that just two-thirds are reported to be users of alcoholic beverages and one-third abstainers (Table 16). This compares with 80% of the male college students who are users. Taking all the mothers in the study, 48% are users compared with 61% of the female college students. These differences in incidence of drinking are consistent with previous studies which found that the incidence among both men and women tended to decrease with advancing age beyond the twenties.[1] We do not know to what extent this reflects a cessation of drinking with advancing age or to what extent it means that fewer of the people in this older generation ever drank.

As in the case of drinking by the students themselves, there is a definite relationship between the incidence of use by parents and family income (Table 16). In the lowest income bracket only 53%

Table 16: Drinking by Parents of College Students, according to Family Income (in per cent)

Fathers	All Fathers	Under $2,500	By Family Income $2,500– $4,999	$5,000– $9,999	$10,000 and over
Abstainer	33	47	38	31	20
User	67	53	62	69	80
Total	100	100	100	100	100

Mothers	All Mothers	Under $2,500	By Family Income $2,500– $4,999	$5,000– $9,999	$10,000 and over
Abstainer	52	72	61	45	32
User	48	28	39	55	68
Total	100	100	100	100	100

of the fathers drink compared with 80% in the highest income group; only 28% of the mothers compared with 68%.

There is also a significant relationship between income and the beverages used by parents. In Table 17 users are divided according to whether they include distilled spirits among their drinks or take only beer or wine. The percentage of those drinking only beer or wine varies with family income, ranging for men from 25% of those in the under $2,500 income bracket down to only 8% of those

1. H. A. Ley, Jr., "The Incidence of Smoking and Drinking among 10,000 Examinees," *Proceedings of the Life Extension Examiners, 2* (1940), 57–63; also J. W. Riley, Jr., and Charles F. Marden, "The Social Pattern of Alcoholic Drinking," *Quarterly Journal of Studies on Alcohol, 8* (September 1947), 263–273.

with incomes of $10,000 or more; and for women from 45% to 11%. These differences may in part reflect the differential cost of the beverages. Or they may reflect variations in the drinking customs

Table 17: Beverage Used by Parents Who Drink, according to Family Income (in per cent)

	All Fathers	By Family Income		
		Under $2,500	$2,500–$4,999	$5,000–$9,999	$10,000 and over
Fathers Who Drink					
Use beer or wine only	14	25	18	11	8
Use spirits	86	75	82	89	92
Total	100	100	100	100	100

	All Mothers	By Family Income		
		Under $2,500	$2,500–$4,999	$5,000–$9,999	$10,000 and over
Mothers Who Drink					
Use beer or wine only	23	45	30	22	11
Use spirits	77	55	70	78	89
Total	100	100	100	100	100

of different social status groups in the society, with income merely one measure of them. This last suggestion is supported by a consideration of choice of drink according to fathers' occupation. Fathers' occupations were classified into 5 groups according to social status. It was found that among men with the highest status jobs only 7% of the users restricted their drinking to beer or wine, as compared with 23% of those in the lower status jobs. The whole question of choice of drink in relation to other factors will be discussed more fully in the next chapter when we consider the types of beverage preferred and those most frequently used by students themselves.

The ratio of drinkers to abstainers among parents also shows a marked relationship to level of educational attainment, especially for mothers (Table 18). Riley and Marden reported a similar finding based on a comparison of persons who had and had not graduated from high school.

If we were to assume the same relationship between probability of drinking and level of education among all young people of 17 to 23 that we have found for the parents of college students, we would conclude that a greater percentage of college students drink than of their contemporaries who do not attend college. Without studying the noncollege group, we have no way of knowing how

Table 18: Drinking by Parents, according to Level of Education (in per cent)

	Level of Education		
Fathers	*Elementary (1–8 grades)*	*High School (9–12 grades)*	*College (13 grades or more)*
Abstainer	36	36	30
User	64	64	70
Total	100	100	100

	Level of Education		
Mothers	*Elementary (1–8 grades)*	*High School (9–12 grades)*	*College (13 grades or more)*
Abstainer	68	56	38
User	32	44	62
Total	100	100	100

many of them drink or abstain. But we have observed a relationship between drinking and income, and it is obvious that families of means are better able to afford a college education for sons or daughters; hence it is reasonable to conclude that the college population contains a higher percentage of drinkers than the noncollege population. Even so, care should be taken to avoid suggesting a cause-and-effect relationship. It does seem safe to say that there is more drinking among segments of our population that send sons and daughters to college than among those who do not.

The influence of parental drinking practices upon those of sons and daughters cannot be stressed too strongly. It appears time and again in the present study.

Of sons who are users 74% report that their fathers drink; of sons who abstain only 35% report their fathers drink; of sons who are users 54% report that their mothers drink; of sons who are abstainers, only 19% (Table 19).

Of sons who report that their fathers use spirits, 91% drink themselves, compared with 78% of those whose fathers use only beer or wine and 60% of those whose fathers abstain. Of sons who report that their mothers drink spirits, 94% drink themselves, compared with 86% of those sons whose mothers drink only beer or wine and 68% of those whose mothers abstain (Table 20).

Table 19: Drinking by Parents, according to Practice of Sons (in per cent)

	Fathers	
Sons	User	Abstainer
Use	74	26
Abstain	35	65

	Mothers	
Sons	User	Abstainer
Use	54	46
Abstain	19	81

Daughters, too, follow the example of their parents. Of daughters who drink, 86% report that their fathers drink, while of daughters who abstain only 42% report use by their fathers; of daughters who drink 72% report that their mothers drink; of daughters who abstain only 22% (Table 21).

Of daughters who report that their fathers use spirits, 80% drink themselves compared with 46% of those whose fathers use only beer or wine and 27% of those whose fathers abstain. Of

Table 20: Drinking by Sons, according to Practice of Parents (in per cent)

	Sons	
Fathers	Use	Abstain
Use spirits	91	9
Use only beer or wine	78	22
Abstain	60	40

	Sons	
Mothers	Use	Abstain
Use spirits	94	6
Use only beer or wine	86	14
Abstain	68	32

daughters who report that their mothers use spirits, 88% drink themselves, compared with 61% of those whose mothers drink only beer or wine and 33% of those whose mothers abstain (Table 22).

Table 21: Drinking by Parents,
according to Practice of
Daughters (in per cent)

	Fathers	
Daughters	*User*	*Abstainer*
Use	86	14
Abstain	42	58

	Mothers	
Daughters	*User*	*Abstainer*
Use	72	28
Abstain	22	78

Parents' attitudes toward drinking by their sons and daughters are also closely related to the parents' own drinking practices. Students who drink and whose drinking was known to their parents were asked to indicate whether they felt that their father and mother approved or disapproved of their drinking, and how strongly. Table 23 indicates that parents who themselves abstain are perceived as predominantly disapproving of their children's drinking. Parents who themselves drink appear much more likely

Table 22: Drinking by Daughters, ac-
cording to Practice of Parents (in
per cent)

	Daughters	
Fathers	*Use*	*Abstain*
Use spirits	80	20
Use only beer or wine	46	54
Abstain	27	73

	Daughters	
Mothers	*Use*	*Abstain*
Use spirits	88	12
Use only beer or wine	61	39
Abstain	33	67

to approve of drinking by a son or a daughter. These contrasts are particularly impressive at the levels of extreme attitude. Fathers who abstain are seen as 7.5 times more likely to disapprove strongly of their sons' drinking than fathers who drink themselves. Fathers who drink appear six times more likely to approve fully of drink-

Table 23: Parents' Attitudes toward Student Drinking, according to Parents' Own Drinking Practice (in per cent)

Fathers' Attitudes toward Drinking by Sons	All Fathers	Father Abstainer	Drinker
Strongly disapprove	8	30	4
Mildly disapprove	37	43	36
Partially approve	34	23	35
Approve	21	4	25
Total	100	100	100

Fathers' Attitudes toward Drinking by Daughters	All Fathers	Father Abstainer	Drinker
Strongly disapprove	5	27	3
Mildly disapprove	30	46	29
Partially approve	26	18	27
Approve	39	9	41
Total	100	100	100

Mothers' Attitudes toward Drinking by Sons	All Mothers	Mother Abstainer	Drinker
Strongly disapprove	18	33	11
Mildly disapprove	43	52	39
Partially approve	22	9	27
Approve	17	6	23
Total	100	100	100

Mothers' Attitudes toward Drinking by Daughters	All Mothers	Mother Abstainer	Drinker
Strongly disapprove	9	31	5
Mildly disapprove	32	42	30
Partially approve	27	15	29
Approve	32	12	36
Total	100	100	100

ing by a son than fathers who abstain. Similar contrasts appear in fathers' attitudes toward drinking by daughters and mothers' attitudes toward drinking by both sons and daughters.

At first glance these figures present an amazing contrast in parental attitudes toward drinking by sons as compared with those toward drinking by daughters. A greater percentage of both fathers and mothers object (mildly, strongly, or both) to their sons' drinking than to their daughters'. This would seem to imply a double standard, which is hardly surprising, but that the double standard should be in favor of daughters' drinking as against sons' is indeed a paradox. To anticipate a later chapter, it may be reported that the girls manifest another equally surprising paradox; they lead the boys approximately two to one in preferring and using distilled spirits as compared to beer or wine.

Findings such as these are not uncommon in phenomena relating to alcoholic beverages, about which there is so much confusion and conflict in our society. However, recognizing some closely related facts largely clears up the apparent paradox. Any superficial impression arising from these two unexpected findings that heavy drinking by college girls is usual and meets with their parents' approval is completely unrealistic. It has already been pointed out (Chapter 5) that girls are more responsive to negative parental sanctions than are boys. Since fewer girls drink against their parents' advice, it follows that fewer girls who drink (as contrasted to boys) would be conscious of parental disapproval of their drinking.

Students were asked whether they knew of "instances of repeated extreme drinking" among members of their family and close friends. A third (31% of the women and 36% of the men) reported intimate acquaintance with a problem drinker. Eight per cent reported repeated extreme drinking by a parent (6.8% of the women, 8.5% of the men). Since most of the students have two parents living, the rate of problem drinking among parents can be calculated at 4%. This figure can be viewed against estimates which place the number of problem drinkers in the United States at approximately four million persons or roughly 4% of the adult population. This rather crude calculation suggests at least that the report from students on prevalence of problem drinking among parents is consistent with the usually accepted estimates for the general population.

The awareness of problem drinking in a parent has certainly not acted as a deterrent to student drinking. Of the men who reported a problem-drinking parent 89% were themselves users, as compared with 78% of all others; of the women, 69% compared with 57%. This relationship poses serious questions for those responsible for education, whether of young persons or adults, whether in a formal setting such as church or school or in an informal setting. The questions relate not only to drinking but to any other customary activities correlated with dangerous or disapproved behavior. Does a negative opinion or command, reinforced by "horrible example," by itself function effectively to change behavior or attitude?

There is much evidence, on a rather superficial level, that many individuals and organizations believe the threat of disease or disaster backed up by examples will cause a change in behavior. A great deal of commercial advertising, as well as slogans, literature, films, and other materials stemming from groups such as health organizations, indicates faith in the efficacy of this kind of approach. Perhaps efforts to change drinking behavior are the most obvious example of all. Two aspects of the relationship of incidence of drinking by a college boy or girl to the presence of a problem-drinker parent should be emphasized. First, the intelligence level of college boys and girls is above average. Second, the impact of problem drinking can be felt far more intensely through experience with such a drinker than through words or pictures, particularly if a young person's relationship to the problem drinker is socially and emotionally very close. The facts presented here indicate that even the actual, emotionally significant, and ever present "awful" example had no effect of decreasing drinking. In fact, there was actually a greater incidence of drinking under such conditions. We do not mean to suggest that techniques utilizing fear, warning, and bad example are useless. We do suggest, however, that by themselves such techniques may be without value, and also that as major tools for modifying behavior they should be viewed with skepticism.

Summary

A review of parents' drinking practices, particularly as they are related to students' own drinking behavior, has revealed several significant facts. The example of parents in drinking or abstaining is seen to be closely correlated with the decision of students to drink or abstain. Parental sanctions against drinking are much more effective than formal sanctions stemming from church or school; and parents' attitudes toward drinking by a son or daughter are usually in line with their own practices. The incidence of problem drinking among parents of college students appears consistent with generally accepted estimates on rates of alcoholism in the entire adult population. Finally, the example of a problem-drinking parent has not acted as a deterrent to drinking by students; and the implications of this finding to an evaluation of fear techniques often employed in education have been suggested.

We have already seen in Chapter 4 that the majority of students who drink started their drinking before entering college. The relation of parental example to student drinking demonstrated in the present chapter further confirms that going to college is not in itself a major influence in determining whether or not students will drink.

More important still, the relationship between parental drinking and students' decisions about drinking strongly emphasizes the fact that drinking is primarily a form of custom, deep set in the culture pattern of certain segments of our population. An individual's participation or nonparticipation in the custom is strongly influenced by the behavior prevailing in his own cultural group.

CHAPTER 7. *What Do Students Drink?*

The description and analysis of student drinking patterns have been presented up to this point largely in terms of users and abstainers. Certain distinctions between members of these two categories have been illustrated by differences in other behavior and attitudes and in various types of group membership. However, division into these two categories is based upon oversimplification, especially in the case of the "users." Abstainers can perhaps be subdivided rather simply into two groups; those who have always abstained and those who adopted abstinence after some experience of drinking. Users cannot be so easily described. The very different pictures suggested by such phrases as occasional user for medicinal purposes, connoisseur of fine wines, Skid Row derelict, the cocktail set, student beer drinker, ritual user of sacramental wine, quart-a-day man, and the like give ample evidence of the wide range of behavior and attitudes merged in the single category of users. Three of the more obvious ways of distinguishing users relate to the amount usually consumed, the frequency of drinking, and the type of beverage. The last of these is the subject of the present chapter.

The more common beverages containing alcohol can be classified in three groups: beer, wine, and distilled spirits. Aside from basic differences in manufacturing processes, these three types of beverage also are characterized by widely varying alcohol content. Beer usually contains from 3 to 6% alcohol by volume. The alcohol content of wines may range from around 8% for some homemade varieties to 12% for common commercial brands of table wines and from 18 to 21% for the aperitifs (sherry, vermouth) which have been fortified by the introduction of distilled alcohol during their manufacture. Distilled spirits contain from around 30 to 50% alcohol by volume. Spirits are commonly classified by their "proof" value, which is approximately twice their alcohol content. A "90 proof" liquor is 45% absolute alcohol.

The price paid for these different types of alcoholic beverage bears some direct relationship to their alcohol content. A quart of beer costs much less than a quart of wine of comparable quality, and a quart of spirits is considerably more expensive than the wine. If we consider just the total beverage content, beer is the cheapest and spirits the most expensive of alcoholic beverages. However, if we consider merely absolute alcohol content, the less expensive brands of spirits and reinforced wines are the cheapest way to buy absolute alcohol in beverage form.

Beer, wines, and spirits are also differentiated by very distinctive tastes. It is not impossible for an individual to acquire a liking for the taste of one form of alcoholic beverage and find other forms quite distasteful.

These major varieties of alcoholic beverage are also distinctive in terms of symbolic values ascribed to them by different cultural groups. Wine, particularly, is associated with a great number of traditional usages. For some religious groups, such as Orthodox Jews, it has an important symbolic meaning and plays a part in formal ritualistic observance. For southern European groups, particularly Italians, it has dietary significance. In most Italian homes wine is served with all meals and is considered a basic part of the daily diet. The use of wine became especially vital to groups living in areas where water was scarce at certain times of year and where pollution made it undesirable for drinking purposes. As the principal liquid item of diet, wine became associated not only with nutrition but with general health and the daily routine of family life.

Whisky and brandy (both distilled spirits) are sometimes accorded medicinal values along with wine. The practice, once followed by many physicians, of prescribing alcohol in connection with various ailments is no longer very common but the usage continues, based as we have said primarily on deep-rooted folk beliefs.

Symbolic usages for beer derive largely from fraternal practices. In addition, certain ethnic groups in the United States, notably Italians, are today substituting beer for wine and ascribing to beer drinking some of the symbolic rationale formerly associated with their use of wine.

There are many factors, then, which may influence an individual's preference for or use of a particular type of alcoholic beverage. These include cost, alcohol content, taste, and traditional customs and beliefs of one's cultural group.

Students who drink were asked to indicate their preference among beer, wine, and distilled spirits (including mixed drinks), as well as which of these types they most frequently use.

Among the men 47% prefer beer, 11% wines, and 42% spirits. Preference by no means dictates use, however. Fully 72% reported that they most frequently use beer, 7% wine, and only 21% spirits. Thus, of the men who prefer spirits, only half drink them most frequently.

Direct correlations of preference and use reveal that

1) of the men who prefer beer, nearly all (96%) most frequently use beer;

2) of the men who prefer wine, only four out of ten (39%) most frequently use wine, 14% use spirits, and nearly half (47%) most frequently use beer;

3) of the men who prefer spirits, just 50% most frequently use spirits while nearly all the others (48%) use beer.

In terms of use:

1) of the men most frequently using spirits the vast majority (87%) prefer spirits, only 7% prefer beer and 6% wine;

2) of the men who tend to use wine, four out of five (79%) prefer wine, only 3% prefer beer, and 18% spirits;

3) of the men most frequently using beer, less than two-thirds (64%) prefer beer, 7% prefer wine, and nearly a third (29%) prefer spirits.

Men who prefer beer usually drink beer, and so do almost half of those who prefer wine or spirits. Most men who use spirits or wine prefer these beverages, but more than a third of the beer users prefer other beverages.

Altogether, 70% of the men reported preferring the beverage that they use most frequently. Among the rest, two out of three prefer spirits but use beer, and these comprise 20% of all the men reporting.

The distribution of men according to family income and type of beverage most frequently used certainly does not substantiate the argument that choice of beverage is dictated by income (Table 24). Actually the lowest income group (below $2,500) has the second

Table 24: Type of Beverage Most Frequently Used by Men, according to Family Income (in per cent)

Family Income	Men Who Most Frequently Use			
	Beer	Wine	Spirits	Total
Under $2,500	67	7	26	100
$2,500–$4,999	74	5	21	100
$5,000–$9,999	73	4	23	100
$10,000 and over	64	4	32	100

highest percentage of users of spirits and the second lowest percentage of beer users. Furthermore, the range of users of any type of beverage shows comparatively little variation between the different income groups.

Although income appears to have little direct influence on the types of beverage used by students as a whole, it is still possible that the practices of some students are determined by the economic factor. If so, this certainly should be apparent for those men who indicated a preference for the more expensive spirits and yet usually drank the less expensive beers. In Table 25 men who indicated a

Table 25: Family Income for Men Who Prefer Distilled Spirits but Usually Drink Beer and for Those Who Both Prefer and Usually Drink Spirits (in per cent)

Family Income	Men Who Prefer Distilled Spirits and Most Frequently Use	
	Spirits	Beer
Under $2,500	16	8
$2,500–$4,999	29	44
$5,000–$9,999	24	27
$10,000 and over	31	21
Total	100	100

preference for distilled spirits but most frequently drank beer (20% of the total male sample reporting) and those who listed spirits as first in both preference and use (21% of the total male sample reporting) are compared according to family income. It is seen that 31% of those who prefer and use spirits are in the top income group, as compared with only 21% of those who use beer although they prefer spirits. However, 16% of those who use spirits are in the lowest income group, compared with only 8% of the beer users. Again there is no basis for explaining differences between beverages preferred and those used by a cost-income theory. It should be noted that the effect of being in the top or bottom income groups is modified by the feeling of being poor or rich. Obviously, feeling "poor" or "rich" is relative to many factors other than income. The high income student may be kept poor buying gasoline for his car. The low income student may enjoy unwonted luxury in college thanks to the sacrifice of proud parents.

A relationship between cost-income and type of beverage used was found for one group of men: those who drink relatively frequently and in larger amounts. Students using beer and spirits were compared, by means of the index of quantity and frequency to be described in Chapter 8, according to family income and their quantity-frequency index rating. For those in the lower indices there were no marked differences in family income distribution between beer and spirits users. But among students with an index of 5 (those who drink more frequently than once a week and on each occasion consume more than 3 ounces of spirits or more than 24 ounces of beer) 56% of the spirits users have family incomes of $10,000 or more, as compared with only 32% of the beer users. For those who consume the most, economic means may be a factor in determining ability to buy drinks containing distilled spirits, but for the lighter drinkers family income bears no relationship to the types of beverage used.

An examination was made to determine whether choice of beverage was related to reasons for drinking. As shown in Chapter 5 certain reasons for drinking are more closely related than others to psychological and physiological effects induced by alcohol. The question arises, therefore, whether students who feel that the effect of alcohol is an important reason for drinking are more apt to use spirits which provide alcohol in the more concentrated form. Actually, there was a striking similarity of response from beer and spirits users on the importance of selected "reasons" for drinking (Table 26). The greatest discrepancy in percentage was for the

Table 26: Per Cent of Male Students Ascribing Importance to Each of 12 Reasons for Drinking, by Type of Beverage Most Frequently Used

Reason for Drinking	Students Who Most Frequently Use		
	Beer	Wine	Spirits
	(per cent ascribing some or considerable importance to each reason)		
To get along better on dates	36	15	36
To relieve fatigue or tension	56	47	55
To be gay	66	41	63
To relieve illness or physical discomfort	26	26	28
To comply with custom	65	53	66
Because of enjoyment of taste	77	65	72
In order not to be shy	27	26	24
As an aid in meeting crises	8	12	12
For a sense of well-being	18	21	28
As an aid in forgetting disappointments	29	18	23
To get high	53	24	42
To get drunk	16	9	17

item "to get high," which 11% more beer drinkers than the spirits users selected as important. For 9 of the 12 items no more than 4 percentage points separated the responses of beer and spirits users. Students who most frequently use wine were generally more apt to check "no importance" next to the various reasons for drinking. Oddly enough, although wine drinking is a deep-rooted custom of many cultural groups, fewer wine drinkers than others felt that complying with custom was an important reason for their drinking. The word "complying" connotes a conscious effort to fit a pattern, and wine for many of these students is so much a part of their diet or customary daily routine that they may not think of drinking as "complying" with anything. Had this item read "as a part of custom" it is possible that most of the wine users would have made a positive response. Wine drinkers approached or equaled users of beer and spirits in ascribing importance to certain items connoting physical or psychological relief, such as "to relieve illness or discomfort," "for a sense of well-being," "in order not to be shy," and "as an aid in meeting crises." They tended to reject reasons suggesting motivations which were partly social or were concerned with intensity of effect.

Another possible explanation for an individual's choice of beverage is related to alcohol content. One might expect students who are seeking the greatest physical or psychological effect from alcohol to be most likely to drink spirits. However, the facts do not bear out this theory. Student users of each type of beverage were compared according to several measures of extent of drinking, including an index of quantity and frequency (Chapter 8), a social complications scale [1] (Chapter 12), number of times drunk, and two questions on behavior suggesting greater than normal stress on the importance of drinking. In all of these comparisons wine users are markedly differentiated from beer and spirits users, but the latter show remarkable similarities. In Table 27 only 12% of the wine users have high quantity-frequency indices (4 or 5), as compared with 43% of the spirits drinkers and 48% of the beer users. Stu-

Table 27: Type of Beverage Used, by Quantity-Frequency Index (in per cent)

Quantity-frequency Index	Male Students Who Most Frequently Use		
	Beer	Wine	Spirits
1 (low)	22	43	18
2–3 (medium)	30	45	39
4–5 (high)	48	12	43
Total	100	100	100

dents having a social complications scale rating of zero (no complications) include 82% of the wine users but less than two-thirds of the beer and spirits users (Table 28). Only 30% of the wine

1. The social complications scale is a measure of difficulties associated with drinking, such as failure to meet certain obligations, damage to friendships, accident or injury, etc.

drinkers have ever been drunk, as compared with 57% of the spirits users and 69% of the beer drinkers (Table 29). A question on anticipatory drinking, "Do you ever drink before going to a party if not sure of getting any drinks or enough to drink?" was

Table 28: Type of Beverage Used, by Social Complications Scale (in per cent)

Social Complications Scale	Male Students Who Most Frequently Use		
	Beer	Wine	Spirits
0 (no complications)	63	82	65
1–2 (infrequent complications)	30	15	27
3–4 (more frequent complications)	7	3	8
Total	100	100	100

answered in the affirmative by a third of the beer users, 26% of the spirits users, and only 6% of those most frequently drinking wine. A question on surreptitious drinking, "Do you like to be one

Table 29: Type of Beverage Used, by Times Drunk (in per cent)

Times Drunk	Male Students Who Most Frequently Use		
	Beer	Wine	Spirits
Never	31	70	43
One to 5 times	50	19	43
More than 5 times	19	11	14
Total	100	100	100

or two drinks ahead without the others knowing it?" was answered yes by 13% of the beer users, 10% of those usually using spirits, and only 3% of the wine drinkers.

Two factors stand out in these data. First, although beer averages around 4.5% alcohol and distilled spirits anywhere from 30 to 50% alcohol, male students who most frequently use beer actually show almost as high or higher quantity-frequency and social complications ratings, have more often been drunk, and are more apt to provide affirmative answers to questions on anticipatory drinking and sneaking of drinks than the drinkers of distilled spirits. Second, few wine users, as measured by all of these ratings, drink for the effect received from alcohol. These data certainly do not suggest that alcohol content as it contributes to effect from drinking is important in the students' choice of type of beverage.

Another possible explanation of choice of beverage is the factor of taste. It has been shown in Chapter 5 that of 13 selected reasons for drinking taste was most frequently cited as important. However, as Table 30 shows, there was no differentiation in the ratings of taste made by the students who most frequently use each of the beverage types. So it seems doubtful that taste is actually a primary factor in the choice of a particular type of beverage.

Table 30: Type of Beverage Used, by Rating of Taste as a Reason for Drinking (in per cent)

| | Male Students Who Most Frequently Use | | |
Rating of Taste	Beer	Wine	Spirits
Considerable importance	30	27	29
Some importance	44	45	44
No importance	26	28	27
Total	100	100	100

There is a suggestion of a limited amount of parental influence in beverage choice. Twenty-seven per cent of the men who reported that their fathers use distilled spirits listed spirits as their own most frequent drink, compared with 17% of those who reported that their fathers drank only beer or wine and 19% of those who indicated that their fathers were abstainers.

There are some differences in beverage choice among the ethnic or cultural groups, but none of these are particularly sharp. In general, among men beer was used more by students of Scandinavian, German, Irish, and French origin than by other ethnic groups; wine by students of Jewish, Italian, and Negro origin more than by the others; while distilled spirits had the greatest percentage of users among those of American nationality background as well as among Negro and Jewish students. The range of variation is not enough to suggest that ethnic factors have major significance.

We are left with the conclusion that choice of beverage among college students is determined primarily by social group associations and by the social context in which drinking takes place. This is supported by consideration of the usual drinking companions of male students according to the type of beverage most frequently used. Table 31 shows that 71% of the beer drinkers usually drink

Table 31: *Type of Beverage Used, by Usual Drinking Companions for Men (in per cent)*

	Male Students Who Most Frequently Use		
Usual Drinking Companions	Beer	Wine	Spirits
Family members	8	51	8
Males only	71	20	30
Females only	4	7	10
Mixed company	16	21	51
Self	1	1	1
Total	100	100	100

in the company of male companions, compared with only 20% of the wine users and 30% of those drinking spirits. Family members are the drinking companions of half the wine users and of only 8% each of those usually using beer or spirits. At the same time half of the spirits users drink in mixed company, but only a fifth of the wine users and even fewer of the beer drinkers. Here are rather dramatic and significant differences. We see that beer drinking is associated with all-male fellowship activities, that wine drinking is most frequently a family affair, and that the consumption of spirits most often occurs in the mixed social group. Of all the factors that we have examined in connection with choice of type of beverage (cost, alcohol content, taste, ethnic group, and social group), only the social group context reveals an outstanding association.

At this point it is appropriate to consider the women in our study. Some very pronounced differences were found in both preference and actual use of different types of beverage by women as compared with men (Table 32).

Women are much less apt to prefer beer, more apt to prefer wine and spirits. As with men, more women use beer than prefer it, while the use of wine and spirits is less than the preference.

It seems curious that college women who drink are much more apt to use beverages containing the greatest amounts of alcohol than are men.

Direct correlations of preference and use reveal that

1) of the women who prefer beer 94% use beer most frequently and 6% use spirits;

2) of the women who prefer wine, but half use it most often, 29% use beer, and 21% spirits;

3) of the women who prefer spirits two-thirds (68%) most frequently use spirits, 1% wine, and 31% beer.

Considered in terms of use:

1) of the women who generally use beer, only one-third (33%) prefer it, just half prefer spirits, and 17% prefer wine;

2) of the women who most often use wine, the majority (93%) prefer it, while 7% prefer spirits;

3) of the women who usually drink spirits 88% prefer it, 10% would rather have wine, and 2% beer.

Table 32: Types of Beverage Preferred and
Types Most Frequently Used by Men
and Women Students Who Drink (in
per cent)

	Beverage of First Preference		Beverage of Most Frequent Use	
	Men	Women	Men	Women
Beer	47	17	72	41
Wine	11	25	7	16
Spirits	42	58	21	43
Total	100	100	100	100

Altogether 68% of the women usually drink the beverage of their preference. Most of the others (19%) prefer spirits but drink beer.

It can be demonstrated that, just as with men, college women's choice of beverage is influenced primarily by factors of association. The figures which show that women drinkers are much more apt than men to use the high alcohol-content spirits can be explained by differences in usual drinking companions of the two sexes.

We see from Table 31 that the majority of male students who usually drink beer do so in male company, while most of those drinking spirits do so in mixed company. In contrast most women, both the beer and the spirits users, usually drink in mixed company. Women who most frequently use wine, like men, are more apt to drink with family members (Table 33).

Furthermore, when men and women are compared according to response to the question "When drinking are you usually in mixed company?" (Table 34) 87% of the women but only 42% of the

Table 33: Type of Beverage Used, by Usual Drinking Companions for Women (in per cent)

Usual Drinking Companions	Female Students Who Most Frequently Use		
	Beer	Wine	Spirits
Family members	12	68	13
Males only	14	6	13
Females only	14	5	5
Mixed company	60	21	69
Total	100	100	100

men are found to drink in mixed company always or usually; only 6% of the women—but six times that many men—drink in mixed company less than half the time.

Table 34: Drinking in Mixed Company, by Men and Women Students (in per cent)

Drinking in Mixed Company	Men	Women
Always	14	39
On most occasions	28	48
About half the time	22	7
Less than half the time	36	6
Total	100	100

We are left with the following picture. Most drinking by college women is in mixed groups. Men, in addition to drinking in mixed social groups, drink even more frequently in all-male fellowships. In the latter the usual beverage is beer, in the former it is more likely to be spirits. In fact, there is a direct correlation between frequency of drinking in mixed company and probability that distilled spirits will be the most frequently used beverage. Men who always or usually drink in mixed company are twice as apt to use spirits as those who drink in mixed company less than half the time. Women, most of whom usually drink in mixed groups, use spirits to a much greater extent than beer. Even when they do drink beer, it is usually in the company of men.

The beer drinking fellowship is a very real and significant factor in the drinking patterns of American male college students. It is common to every type of college studied, with the possible exception of Negro colleges in the South. It undoubtedly traces from customs common for centuries in European universities, but today it is very much an American custom.

Summary

Reiteration of the warning that the data of this study do not come from the total population but from one segment of a particular age range can become wearisome, but the tendency to generalize is so natural that repetition is necessary.

In the matter of types of beverage used, one clear difference between male college students and older men indicates the danger of swift analogy. Among business and professional groups, especially in the larger cities, drinking distilled spirits before meals is common, particularly at meetings primarily of a business nature. For a great number of men this usually all-male drinking may well be the typical or even dominant pattern. Although we have not collected data on this phenomenon, casual observation and common report indicate that beer is rarely if ever the beverage used in this setting. There appears to be no common drinking practice of college students similar to this apparently widespread use of hard liquor in the business-professional world. Furthermore, all-male beer drinking appears to decrease following graduation from college. Thus it seems highly probable that the degree of differences in type of beverage consumed, according to the user's sex, would not be the same for the older population as for those in college. (This is not to suggest that all differences in choice of beverage according to sex would disappear.)

It is noteworthy that students' choice of beverage appears unrelated to several of the factors which were found to be associated with the over-all question of use or abstinence. These factors, such as family income, religion, and ethnic group, are largely beyond the control of the individual. Instead, variations in choice were seen to accompany such factors as drinking situation or drinking companions, matters which are more subject to individual control.

Generally speaking, specific aspects of a custom (such as type of beverage used in drinking) are more flexible and change with greater ease than over-all customs, such as drinking or abstinence. It is also common in cultural change to find that considerable variation in many specific details of the custom may take place while the over-all conceptualization of the custom and attitudes toward the custom remain static.

Just such a situation may be seen in the attitude toward drinking in relation to the type of beverage used. In the period between 1830 and 1850 more than 90% of all alcohol consumed in the United States was in the form of distilled spirits. Many attitudes and concepts which then developed about "drinking" became embedded in religious, legal, educational, and other contexts. By 1950, however, only 40% of all alcohol was consumed in the form of distilled spirits—and in addition, the number and categories of people drinking and the amounts usually consumed had also changed markedly. These changes within the pattern were not accompanied by corresponding changes in attitude toward the over-all pattern of drinking alcoholic beverages.

Much of the conflict between Wets and Drys and much of the confusion to be found in individual attitudes about drinking stem from this marked distinction between actual behavior in the 1950's and the beliefs about this behavior which in large part derive from mid-19th-century observation and practice. It is only through knowledge of such matters as the amount and frequency of drinking that it becomes possible to understand what is comprised within such a sweeping concept as "drinking," what is the realistic area of so-called problems, and what aspects of drinking behavior may be more susceptible to rationally planned change.

CHAPTER 8. *How Much and How Often?*

For a great many people in the United States the words drink and drinker carry implications of drunkenness, debauchery, accidents, violence, and disgrace. This implication, or the explicit association of such conditions with drinking or with alcohol itself, can be seen in statutes requiring that schools teach children about the evils of alcohol, in sermons and official church documents of most Protestant denominations, and in newspaper headlines about accidents and crimes involving excessive drinking. Associating drinking with various evils has been encouraged by militant "dry" associations, in whose eyes, of course, any and all drinking is excessive. When we add to these associations and ideas the fact that youth often appears irresponsible and foolish to the older generation, it is not surprising to find that the word drinking used in connection with college students is apt to convey an impression of excess.

Stereotypes of college drinking include the belief that most students drink, that they do so heavily and frequently, and that dangerous and disgraceful behavior often ensues. These stereotypes are frequently accompanied by courses of action designed to diminish, control, or prevent student drinking. Such controls often meet resistance and sometimes provoke a perverse reaction. This may stem in part from the simple fact that the adult conception of college drinking is very far from reality.

In this chapter we shall consider two basic questions: how frequently do students drink and how much alcohol do they usually consume? We shall also consider the relationships between the frequency and quantity of drinking and such factors as age when drinking started, family income, parental practices, religion, cultural group membership, and certain attitudes about drinking.

For a measure of frequency, students who drink were asked "How often during the past year did you have one or more drinks?" The distribution of replies certainly does not suggest that frequent drinking by students is widespread (Table 35). Over two-fifths of

Table 35: *Frequency of Drinking during Past Year (in per cent)*

Frequency	Users of Alcoholic Beverages	
	Men	Women
1 to 5 times	19	26
6 to 12 times	24	27
Twice a month to once a week	36	37
2 or 3 days a week	18	9
4 or more days a week	3	1
Total	100	100

the men and more than half the women who drink do so no more than once a month. A fifth of the men and a fourth of the women who drink do so less than six times a year. Only 21% of the men and 10% of the women drink oftener than once a week. It is obvious that male student users drink more frequently than female users. It is also obvious that the stereotype of frequent drinking describes a relatively small segment even of the students who drink. Nor is frequency of drinking necessarily related to the life at college. Students were asked to indicate whether they drink on the average more often at college or on vacation. Half the women reported no difference, while the rest divided evenly between college and vacation. Half the men too reported no difference, but 15% reported more frequent drinking at college and 35% more drinking on vacation.

Achieving some estimate of the average amounts of alcohol consumed by students on any particular occasion of drinking was much more complicated. A measure of quantity, in order to be meaningful, depends both on what is drunk and on the approximate absolute alcohol content. Six ounces of beer contains but a tenth as much absolute alcohol as six ounces of straight whisky. Furthermore, people seldom make conscious note of how much they drink in terms of any standard measure. One can usually estimate that he drinks an average of two beers each time, and specify whether he means a glass or a bottle or can. Similarly he may be able to estimate the number of glasses of wine or the number of drinks containing spirits that he usually consumes. But containers vary in size. A wineglass may hold 1.5 or 2 ounces for sherry or 4, 6, or even 8 ounces for some of the table wines. Beer is usually served in 6 or 8 ounce glasses. Drinks containing distilled spirits may be served in almost any size of glass; there is less variation in the actual amount of distilled spirits in the drink but even this may run from 1 to 3 ounces.

In order to approximate the amounts consumed, some standardizing had to be done, and adjustments made for differences in the alcohol content of various types of beverage. The students were merely asked to indicate, for each type of beverage (beer, wine, and spirits), the average amount ordinarily consumed at a sitting, disregarding any extreme experiences. The information thus provided was then coded into three groups arbitrarily labeled as smaller, medium, and larger amounts. Coding criteria were designed so that the various classifications would contain approximately the same amount of absolute alcohol, regardless of beverage type. Smaller amounts would contain less than 1.4 ounces of absolute alcohol; medium amounts between 1.4 and 3 ounces; and larger amounts 3 ounces or more.[1] Translating the terms used by the students, smaller amounts include up to 3 glasses or 2 bottles or cans of beer, up to 2 glasses of wine, or 2 drinks containing spirits; larger amounts include more than 8 glasses or 6 bottles of beer, 6 glasses of wine, or 4 drinks containing spirits. For purposes of approximation, it was assumed that the average wineglass contained 3.5 ounces, the average beer glass 8 ounces, and the average jigger, "shot," or drink containing spirits 1.5 ounces.

The average quantity of alcoholic beverages consumed at a sitting showed rather wide variation depending on the type of beverage

1. Adoption of 1.4 and 3 ounces was based upon pretests of survey procedures and the necessity of arriving at figures by means of which different types of beverages and different types of containers could be reduced to units of absolute alcohol. No value judgment of what constitutes "small" or "large" consumption is involved. The figures merely happen to be useful for analyzing these data.

and the sex of the drinker (Table 36). Both men and women consumed more alcohol at a sitting when drinking spirits than when drinking beer or wine. More than 95% of students of both sexes consumed only smaller or medium amounts of wine, and more than 90% consumed smaller or medium amounts of beer. Three out of

Table 36: Average Amounts of Beer, Wine, and Spirits Consumed at a Sitting (in per cent)

Average Amounts	Men	Women
Beer	Users of Beer	
Smaller	46	73
Medium	45	26
Larger	9	1
Total	100	100
Wine	Users of Wine	
Smaller	79	89
Medium	17	11
Larger	4	— *
Total	100	100
Spirits	Users of Spirits	
Smaller	40	60
Medium	31	33
Larger	29	7
Total	100	100

* <0.5%.

ten men and 7% of the women reported that they usually drink larger amounts of spirits.

Some idea of the effects on behavior which can be expected from given amounts of alcohol can be gained by relating particular amounts to expected blood-alcohol concentration and by considering the level of blood-alcohol concentrations which the National Safety Council has found sufficient to permit the suspicion that drinking might have reduced efficiency in the highly responsible and demanding activity of driving a car.

The Council has proposed, and several states have accepted, the thesis that a concentration of 0.15% shall be considered, for purposes of driving a motor vehicle, a priori evidence of being "under the influence"; that a concentration of less than 0.05% shall be held to be not "under the influence" for driving; and that intermediate concentrations shall be considered a range open to decision.

The college student weighing between 150 and 160 pounds who drank three highballs or cocktails on an empty stomach over a period of two-and-a-half or three hours would achieve a peak alcohol concentration of about 0.06%. If the student were heavier, had recently had a meal, had been eating while drinking or extended his drinking to three-and-a-half or four hours, the concentration in each instance would be less. If he took three drinks at once the concentration might reach 0.09%. Peak concentration would be dissipated at the rate of about 0.02% an hour.

Quite aside from value judgments about driving when drinking (which is under no circumstances to be recommended), our findings do not support the stereotype of heavy drinking by most students. They do indicate that there is a small percentage of students who drink to the point of manifest effect on behavior. Certainly an individual who has consumed three highballs cannot immediately afterward drive a car safely.

In measuring the extent of drinking, neither quantity nor frequency alone provides an adequate index. Even the individual who drinks daily would probably not be considered a heavy drinker if he consumed only a glass of beer or wine or one drink with spirits. Nor would a person be considered a heavy drinker who takes say five drinks at a sitting, if his drinking is confined to three or four specific holidays or events a year. It was deemed desirable to find a measure of drinking which would account for frequency and quantity at the same time.

Following established statistical techniques, we determined indices of quantity and frequency of drinking by men and by women. Quantity values for the indices were taken as the usual amounts consumed of the type of beverage most frequently used. Combinations of five designations for frequency of drinking during the past year and three for quantity provided 15 possible quantity-frequency index types. An examination of these according to several criteria of behavior resulted in their eventual combination into five types for men and two for women.

Descriptions follow of the various index types and the percentage distribution of student drinkers among them. It should be noted that 11% of the men and 5% of the women could not be assigned to a type because certain necessary items of information were not available. These students are therefore excluded from further considerations of quantity and frequency as related to other aspects of behavior.

Male Quantity-Frequency (Q-F) Index	Per Cent Users
Type 1. Drinks infrequently (once a month at the most) and consumes only smaller amounts (not more than approximately 1.3 ounces of absolute alcohol).	24
Type 2. Drinks infrequently and consumes medium or larger amounts (enough to provide more than 1.3 ounces of absolute alcohol).	16
Type 3. Drinks more than once a month but consumes only smaller amounts.	17
Type 4. Drinks two to four times a month and consumes medium or larger amounts.	26
Type 5. Drinks more than once a week and consumes medium or larger amounts.	17
Total	100

Female Quantity-Frequency (Q-F) Index	Per Cent Users
Type 1. Either drinks only infrequently, regardless of amount, or drinks two to four times a month but consumes only smaller amounts.	71
Type 2. Either drinks only two to four times a month but consumes medium or larger amounts, or drinks more than once a week, regardless of amount.	29
Total	100

It should be stressed that the quantity-frequency indices are merely conceptual tools which will be used as convenient measures in considering the relationship between the extent of drinking and various other aspects of behavior.

Age

Consideration of the extent of drinking by students according to their chronological age suggests that a peak in the quantity and frequency of drinking may be reached during college. Men with the two highest Q-F index scores (4 and 5) comprised 35% of those 18 years and under, exactly half of those in the ages 19 to 21, and only 41% of those over 21. Women show a similar curve. Those with a high Q-F index (2) comprise only 16% of the girls 18 years or under, 36% of the 19- to 20-year-old group, a peak of 44% of the 21-year-olds, and only 29% of those over 21.

However, it has been found that chronological age is not the best index of maturation for young people of college age. Because a majority of the students are within the limited age range of 17 to 23, meaningful measures of growth are best made in terms of experience and advancement in social maturation. Thus, other factors being equal, we might expect to find just as great differences in development between a 19-year-old sophomore and a 19-year-old senior as we would between 18- and 20-year-old sophomores.

It was shown in Chapter 4 that the incidence of drinkers increased with each college year, from 69% of the freshmen to 87% of the seniors among men, and from 46% of the freshmen to 77% of the seniors among women.

Among women drinkers there is a similar relationship between college year and extent of drinking (Table 37). Students with the

Table 37: Quantity and Frequency of Drinking by Women, according to College Year (in per cent)

Female Quantity-Frequency Index	Freshman	Sophomore	Junior	Senior
1	84	75	68	52
2	16	25	32	48
Total	100	100	100	100

higher Q-F index (2) increase from 16% of the freshmen to 48% of the seniors. Taken year by year, there is roughly a 50% increase in index 2 women drinkers each college year. Not so striking a relationship appears among men (Table 38). Those with higher

Q-F indices comprise 39% of the freshmen, 46% of the sophomores, 47% of the juniors, and there is then a slight drop to 44% of the seniors.

Table 38: Quantity and Frequency of Drinking by Men, according to College Year (in per cent)

Male Quantity-Frequency Index	Freshman	Sophomore	Junior	Senior
1	29	22	24	21
2	19	11	16	16
3	13	21	13	19
4	28	26	29	22
5	11	20	18	22
Total	100	100	100	100

Even more significant than age itself in relation to the extent of drinking among college students is a relationship to the age at which students started to drink. By and large, the earlier a student began his drinking the greater its extent (Table 39). Among the

Table 39: Quantity-Frequency Index, by Age When Drinking Started (in per cent)

	Age When Drinking Started				
	Before Entering College			After Entering College	
Male Q-F Index	Under 16	16–17	18 and over	Under 20	20 and over
1	14	20	23	30	30
2	12	12	14	16	20
3	12	17	19	16	17
4	29	28	27	26	20
5	33	23	17	12	13
Total	100	100	100	100	100
Female Q-F Index					
1	43	70	80	63	85
2	57	30	20	37	15
Total	100	100	100	100	100

men who first drank before entering college, 62% of those who began drinking before they were 16 had a Q-F rating of 4 or 5.

This compares with only 51% of those who began at ages 16 or 17, and 44% of those who first drank at ages 18 or above. It also can be compared with 38% of those who did not start to drink until after they entered college and were under 20 years of age at that time, and 33% of those who first drank after entering college, at the age of 20 or above. For women the percentages of those with a Q-F index of 2 are also related to age of first drinking.

Similar findings can be reported with respect to the age at which students are first tight (Table 40). Men with Q-F ratings of 4 or 5

Table 40: Quantity-Frequency Index, by Age When First Tight (in per cent)

| | | Students Who Have Been Tight | | | |
| | | Age First Tight | | | Never |
Male Q-F Index		Under 16	16–17	18–19	20 and over	Tight
1		13	21	15	23	48
2		13	15	13	21	19
3		11	15	17	22	18
4		26	27	34	21	11
5		37	22	21	13	4
	Total	100	100	100	100	100
Female Q-F Index						
1		40	39	61	78	81
2		60	61	39	22	19
	Total	100	100	100	100	100

included 63% of those who had been tight and experienced this state before the age of 16 and only 34% of those who had first been tight at the age of 20 or later. Women with a Q-F rating of 2 included 60% of those first tight before age 16, only 22% of those first tight at age 20 or later.

Drinking by Parents

We have already seen that the example of parents seemed closely related to the probability that a student would drink or abstain. Parental example also shows some relationship to the extent to which students will drink (Table 41). Men with a Q-F rating of 4 or 5 include nearly half of those whose parents both drink, and only a third of those whose parents both abstain. Women with a

Q-F rating of 2 include 32% of those whose parents both drink, only 11% where both parents abstain.

Table 41: Quantity-Frequency Index, by Parents' Drinking (in per cent)

Male Q-F Index	Both Parents Drink	One Parent Drinks	Both Parents Abstain
1	22	26	35
2	14	18	19
3	17	13	14
4	29	23	22
5	18	20	10
Total	100	100	100

Female Q-F Index			
1	68	74	89
2	32	26	11
Total	100	100	100

Family Income

Family income, which showed some relationship to the probability that a student would drink or abstain but no direct relationship to choice of type of beverage, appears here as a possible factor in the frequency and extent of drinking (Table 42). Men with a

Table 42: Quantity-Frequency Index, by Family Income (in per cent)

Male Q-F Index	Family Income			
	Under $2,500	$2,500–$4,999	$5,000–$9,999	$10,000 and over
1	29	25	26	18
2	21	17	14	14
3	23	16	18	10
4	15	29	25	29
5	12	13	17	29
Total	100	100	100	100

Female Q-F Index				
1	82	81	65	67
2	18	19	35	33
Total	100	100	100	100

Q-F index of 4 or 5 ranged from 58% of those with family incomes of $10,000 or more down to only 27% of those with family incomes under $2,500. Women with a Q-F index of 2 showed a similar range from 33% down to 18%.

Sex of Drinking Companions

The sex of drinking companions bears a curious relationship to quantity and frequency of drinking. Men who reported that they always or on most occasions drank in mixed company are weighted toward the lower Q-F index ratings, in contrast to those who drank in mixed company half the time or less. College men who usually drink in the company of the opposite sex are less apt to be frequent or heavy drinkers than those who usually drink with other men (Table 43). It will be remembered that fully 87% of the college

Table 43: Quantity-Frequency Index, by Frequency
of Drinking in Mixed Company (in per cent)

| | Drink in Mixed Company | |
| | Always or on Most | Half the Time |
Male Q-F Index	Occasions	or Less
1	29	20
2	17	15
3	17	17
4	24	27
5	13	21
Total	100	100
Female Q-F Index		
1	70	78
2	30	22
Total	100	100

women usually or always drink in mixed company. These are somewhat more apt to be Q-F 2 drinkers than those who seldom or never drink in mixed company.

Beverage Type

When ranked according to the beverage they drink most frequently, more extensive drinkers (Q-F ratings of 4 or 5) are found to include 48% of the men who usually drink beer, 43% of those usually drinking spirits, and only 12% of those drinking wine. Among women, those with a Q-F rating of 2 constituted 36 and 39% respectively of the beer and spirits users and only 11% of the wine drinkers (Table 44).

Table 44: Quantity-Frequency Index, by Beverage Most Frequently Used (in per cent)

	Students Whose Beverage of Most Frequent Use Is		
Male Q-F Index	*Beer*	*Wine*	*Spirits*
1	22	42	18
2	12	3	28
3	18	43	11
4	28	6	27
5	20	6	16
Total	100	100	100
Female Q-F Index			
1	64	89	61
2	36	11	39
Total	100	100	100

Religion and Nationality

The quantity-frequency index also shows some rather revealing differences in the drinking patterns of students who belong to different religions (Table 45). The Catholic men, particularly, appear

Table 45: Quantity-Frequency Index, by Religious Affiliation (in per cent)

	Religious Affiliation			
Male Q-F Index	*Catholic*	*Jewish*	*Mormon*	*Protestant*
1	16	31	33	28
2	17	13	17	14
3	10	22	18	21
4	29	25	25	23
5	28	9	7	14
Total	100	100	100	100
Female Q-F Index				
1	70	75	86	71
2	30	25	14	29
Total	100	100	100	100

to be more frequent and heavier drinkers. Twenty-eight per cent of the Catholics have a Q-F index of 5, compared with only 14% of the Protestants who drink. Only 16% of the Catholics have an index of 1 compared with 28% of the Protestants. Jewish and Mormon male users drink even less than the Protestants. Among women drinkers there are no differences between Catholics and Protestants; Jews drink somewhat less and Mormons the least. It is noteworthy that the Jews, who fall well behind both Catholics and Protestants in extent of drinking, have the greatest percentage of users of alcoholic beverages in their total membership. The Catholic men, who are well ahead in frequency and quantity of drinking, are second to the Jews in incidence of use. Catholic women are well ahead of Protestant women in incidence although they are equal in extent of drinking. There is obviously no direct correlation between incidence of users and extent of drinking by users.

Just as in the case of incidence of drinking, differences in quantity and frequency according to religion in part reflect and in part are reflected by variations in the drinking patterns of certain ethnic and nationality groups. Among the various ethnic groups the Irish men are well ahead of all others in extent of drinking. Fully 62% of the Irish had Q-F ratings of 4 or 5, compared with only about 35% of the Americans, British, and Russians, 44% of the Italians, and 48% of the Germans. Significant differences were not found among women of different nationalities.

The main problem associated with drinking by young people of college age is not alcoholism, which usually takes many years to develop and is relatively rare in young persons; it is intoxication and the many undesirable results of a condition under which the individual fails to retain control over his behavior. Various categories of behavior resulting from the different levels of effect of alcohol will be considered in Chapter 10, and behavior associated with potential problem drinking will be discussed in Chapter 12. Our purpose here is merely to consider the relationship between the extent of drinking, as measured by quantity and frequency, and certain behavior associated with alcohol.

The quantity-frequency indices were related to the number of instances of drunkenness in their life which students reported. Being drunk was defined as "overstepping of social expectancies (short of complete passing out), loss of control in ordinary physical activities, and inability to respond to the reactions of others." As might be expected, a direct correlation is seen between frequency and quantity of drinking and the experience of being drunk (Table 46). Three times as many male students who were never drunk have

Table 46: Quantity-Frequency Index, by Times
Drunk (in per cent)

Male Q-F Index	Never	Once	2 or More Times
	Number of Times Drunk		
1	37	27	13
2	18	22	12
3	17	17	17
4	22	21	31
5	6	13	27
Total	100	100	100
Female Q-F Index			
1	74	44	37
2	26	56	63
Total	100	100	100

a Q-F rating of 1 as students who have been drunk more than once. On the other hand students drunk twice or oftener have a Q-F rating of 5 twice as frequently as students who have been drunk only once, and 4.5 times more often than students who have never been drunk. Somewhat similar relationships are found in the data for women.

In considering potential problem drinking among college students, a number of questions were asked about specific types of behavior which have frequently been recalled by alcoholics as accompanying their earlier drinking experiences. These types of behavior by no means necessarily portend alcoholism. They are sometimes reported by people with no drinking problems. However, they are recalled by alcoholics to an impressive degree. Quantity-frequency indices have been related to two of these questions. One of the questions, "Do you ever drink before going to a party if not sure of getting any drinks or enough to drink?" would probably be answered in the affirmative by many persons who merely like

to drink but have developed no real dependence on alcohol. However, that answer is also a telling mark of one who has begun to
feel a special need of alcohol in order to face certain situations. The
other question, "Do you like to be one or two drinks ahead without
others knowing it?" is perhaps a little more significant. It suggests
that the individual is aware that he drinks more than others, feels
he *has* to drink more than the next fellow, and is responding by
trying to get in extra drinks on the sly. The over-all distribution of
student replies to these and similar questions will be considered in
Chapter 12. Here we are concerned with the relationship of quantity
and frequency of drinking to affirmative or negative replies. And
we find an expected relationship between the extent of drinking
and these indications of special stress on the importance of drinking
(Table 47). Altogether, 81% of the surreptitious (one or two ahead)

*Table 47: Quantity-Frequency Index, by Special Stress on
Drinking (in per cent)*

Male Q-F Index	Drink before a party if not sure of getting any drinks or enough to drink	Like to be one or two drinks ahead without the others knowing it	Neither
1	3	5	33
2	9	8	18
3	13	6	19
4	38	35	20
5	37	46	10
Total	100	100	100

drinkers and 75% of the anticipatory (before a party) drinkers have
a Q-F rating of 4 or 5, as compared with only 30% of those answer-
ing no to both questions. Findings for women are not statistically
significant because relatively few women provide affirmative replies
to the questions, but they indicate the same type of relationship.
    The responses to questions about damaging consequences asso-
ciated with drinking have been subjected to scale analysis and
treated here as a social complications scale (considered more fully
in Chapter 12). For the moment we are merely concerned with the
fact that we have such a scale and that students are rated from zero,
for those who reported no complications whatsoever associated

with their drinking, up to 4 for students who reported experiencing
a number of different complications. Complications included inter-
ference with preparation for classes or examinations, damage to
friendships, loss of jobs, accident or injury, arrest or subjection to
college discipline because of drinking. Quantity and frequency of
drinking were related to position on the social complications scale
for men (Table 48). Of students with high complications scale

Table 48: Quantity-Frequency Index, by Social Complications Scale (in per cent)

		Social Complications Scale	
	0	1-2	3-4
Male Q-F Index	None	Few	More Frequent
1	32	9	4
2	18	13	0
3	18	16	14
4	23	33	29
5	9	29	53
Total	100	100	100

ratings of 3 or 4, only 4% have low Q-F ratings (under 3), compared
with half of those with no complications; and 53% have the highest
Q-F rating, compared with only 9% of those with no complications.

This consideration of effect experienced from alcohol, various
warning signs of potential problem drinking, and complications
associated with drinking, all in relation to the extent of drinking,
leaves little doubt that even in young people of college age problems associated with drinking are directly correlated with both
the amounts of alcohol consumed and the frequency of drinking.
The extent of drinking appears also to be related to various student
attitudes toward drinking. One question on attitude sought a
measure of student opinion on the "extent to which girls of college age should drink" (Table 49). Two-thirds of the male users
and half the females who felt that girls should drink "anything and
as much as they please" had high Q-F ratings, while the majority of
those who would prohibit drinking by girls had low Q-F ratings.
Ratings of students who felt that girls should drink in moderation
provide intermediate measures. There is obviously a close relation-

ship between the extent of a student's own drinking and the degree
of liberality he or she would accord to girls.

Table 49: Quantity-Frequency Index, by Attitude on
    Extent to Which Girls of College Age Should
    Drink (in per cent)

Male Q-F Index	Not at All	Moderation	Anything and As Much As They Please
1	39	20	9
2	26	14	0
3	16	18	24
4	15	28	31
5	4	20	36
Total	100	100	100

Female Q-F Index			
1	100	69	50
2	0	31	50
Total	100	100	100

Summary

Findings on amounts consumed and frequency of drinking indicate clearly that stereotypes of college drinking which include notions of widespread, frequent, and heavy drinking are unrealistic.
The proportion of students who drink frequently and heavily is
very small. Furthermore, even the category of most extensive drinking used in this study (Q-F type 5) includes at its lowest limits
amounts of alcohol which would rarely, if ever, be accompanied
by manifest signs of effect. For example, Q-F type 5 can include
men whose drinking does not exceed three cocktails or four glasses
of beer at any one time and occurs no oftener than twice a week.
For most people not opposed to any or all drinking as such, this
would not be called "heavy" consumption. Obviously, the type 5
category includes students whose consumption pattern greatly exceeds the minimum example just cited. However, even with these
minimal criteria for frequency and amount the type 5 category includes but 17% of the men who drink and 14% of all male students.

Two facts stand out in relation to frequency of drinking. Less than half the students drink more than once a month; fewer than a fifth of the men and than a tenth of the women drink more than once a week.

In terms of quantity, it can be noted that of those who use beer only 9% of the men and 1% of the women usually consume what has arbitrarily been termed "larger" amounts. Of those who drink wine, only 4% of the men and virtually none of the women consume "larger" amounts. Of students who use spirits, 27% of the men and only 7% of the women consume "larger" amounts. Furthermore, a substantial segment of those who use "larger" amounts drink infrequently.

A further comment can be made on the relationship of student drinking to the experience of college. For the more frequent drinkers and for those who drink so-called larger amounts, it is clear that attendance at college is not of major significance in their drinking. These are the students who are most apt to have started drinking before entering college and whose parents are most apt to have approved of their drinking. Male students whose pattern of drinking varies between periods of vacation and actual attendance at college are apt to drink more while on vacation. So it can be concluded that maturation and social background have more influence on the quantity and frequency of drinking than does entrance into college.

In discussing questions of frequency and amount of drinking this chapter has considered "excessive" drinking, and problems related to drinking, only in indirect fashion and only for purposes of interpreting frequency and amount. It should be apparent to every reader that "excess" or "problems" need not be related to greater frequency or greater amounts. The boy or girl who has never before touched alcoholic beverages, who on one occasion takes three drinks, and never again touches liquor may suffer more damage from this one experience than a boy or girl who ordinarily drinks this amount 50 times a year. The matter of problems related to drinking will be considered separately.

CHAPTER 9. *When, Where, with Whom?*

In seeking to describe patterns of drinking behavior by college students, we are looking for frequently recurring combinations of many factors. Other basic factors in the drinking custom besides quantity and frequency are the time, the place, and the companions. Usually these factors are closely related. Drinking in the home is apt to be with family members and most likely at mealtime. Drinking in night clubs is restricted to evening hours and is usually with mixed groups or with one person of the opposite sex.

Childhood Drinking Experience

In considering time factors in drinking we shall include the time when students first started to drink. A significant segment of students experienced some form of drinking in childhood, and it was necessary to distinguish the "onset" of drinking from the experimental sip, the joking incident, or the ceremonial taste sometimes taken as a child.

An attempt was made in the survey to measure the extent of experimental or customary childhood use of alcoholic beverages. Students were asked if they had ever had any alcoholic beverages before the age of 11 as occasional sips, experiment or joke, medicine, on special occasions, or as part of a regular family (social or religious) custom or practice. Altogether, 43% reported such childhood acquaintance with alcohol, boys showing slightly higher percentages than girls (Table 50).

There are rather substantial differences reported in the purposes and occasions of childhood use, according to type of beverage. Since the reports of both sexes were similar, childhood practices of boys and girls are considered together (Table 51). The use of alcohol as a medicine represented 37% of the reported childhood use of distilled spirits but only 8% of the use of wine and 3% of the use of beer. Clearly it is the alcohol and not the other components which is believed to have medicinal efficacy.

Table 50: Use of Alcoholic Beverages in Childhood (in per cent)

Beverage Type	Men	Women	All Students Men and Women
Beer	32	23	29
Wine	33	27	31
Spirits	23	19	22
Some type of alcoholic beverage	45	40	43

Wine is predominantly the alcoholic beverage for children when drinking is part of a regular custom or practice within the family, whether the function is religious or social in nature. Of all the

Table 51: Purposes and Occasions of Childhood Drinking (in per cent)

	Childhood Use of Beer	Wine	Spirits
Occasional sips	62	41	29
As an experiment or a joke	21	11	19
As a medicine	3	8	37
On special occasions	10	19	10
As part of a regular family (social or religious) custom or practice	4	21	5
Total	100	100	100

forms of childhood use of alcohol, that most frequently described is the occasional sip. This accounts for three out of five instances of childhood use of beer and two out of every five occasions when children had tasted wine.

The incidence of childhood familiarity with alcoholic beverages also shows rather sharp variations based on religious and ethnic group membership (Table 52).

There were also cultural differences for childhood drinking in type of beverage used and in drinking occasions. These are in accordance with already observed cultural differences. Jewish and Italian drinkers almost without exception had used wine. In the case of the Jews the great majority had used it in connection with family or religious customs. Italians were more apt to set down their

Table 52: Incidence of Drinking in Childhood, according to Religious and Ethnic Group Membership (in per cent)

By Religion	All Students
Jewish	81
Catholic	54
Protestant	37
Mormon	27

By Ethnic Group (excluding Jews and Mormons)	
Russian	80
Italian	76
German	61
Irish	45
Negro	39
American	34
British	29

early use as occasional sips. About half the German, Russian, and French students also had wine in childhood, again largely in the form of occasional sips. Childhood use of beer was most common among those of German background, exactly half of whom reported tasting it as children primarily as sips or on special occasions. Beer was also mentioned by 43% of the Italian students; as has been remarked, it is often being substituted for the traditional wine by second- and third-generation Italians. There was no great variation in the percentage of students from various cultural groups who reported having used spirits in childhood, except that this included only 13% of the Mormons and 15% each of British and Americans, while other cultural groups ranged for the most part from 25 to 30%. The medicinal usage already noted as the most frequent occasion for childhood use of spirits was particularly prominent with Mormon, French, Russian, and Irish students.

Onset of Postchildhood Drinking

We noted in Chapter 4 that 79% of the men who drink and 65%
of the women reported that their drinking started before entering
college. Of these only 5% of the men and 6% of the women failed
to distinguish present drinking from the childhood pattern. The
distribution of the other students according to age at onset of post-
childhood drinking appears in Table 53. A total of 47% of the

Table 53: Age of Onset of Post-
childhood Drinking (in per
cent)

	Students Who Drink	
Age	Men	Women
11–15	11	9
16–17	36	47
18 and older	53	44
Total	100	100

men who drink and 56% of the women did their first regular
drinking before the age of 18. It is obvious that the "when" of
early drinking for many students antedates their entering college.

Students were also asked to recall the place of their first drinking
beyond the childhood level, and their companions at the time
(Tables 54 and 55). A third of the men and over half the women

Table 54: Place of First Postchildhood
Drinking (in per cent)

	Students Who Drink	
Place	Men	Women
Own home	34	53
Home of a friend	17	14
College building	2	3
Restaurant, tavern, or bar	19	10
Night club	6	12
Automobile	10	2
Private club	3	3
Other (primarily military service for men)	9	3
Total	100	100

reported having their first drink at home. For more than a quarter of the men and half the women, companions were family members. These findings add still further evidence to the already demonstrated influence of parental example and parental sanction on student drinking. Excluding the family, companions at first drink-

Table 55: Companions at First Postchildhood Drinking (in per cent)

Companions	Students Who Drink	
	Men	Women
Family	27	51
Close friends, same sex	53	11
Others, same sex	3	— *
Close friends, opposite sex or mixed group	13	32
Others, opposite sex or mixed group	2	5
Other (includes alone)	2	1
Total	100	100

* $<0.5\%$.

ing were close friends of the same sex for 53% of the boys but for only 11% of the girls; members of the opposite sex for only 13% of the boys but for 32% of the girls. Even with the first drink we see the suggestion of an all-male drinking fellowship and a pattern of girls drinking in mixed company.

Students who had been tight were asked to recall the place and companions. Here the role of the family diminishes: only 5% of the boys and 11% of the girls reported first getting tight in their own homes (Table 56), and only 3 and 7% respectively reported

Table 56: Place of First Becoming Tight (in per cent)

Place	Students Who Have Been Tight	
	Men	Women
Own home	5	11
Home of a friend	17	28
College building	7	10
Restaurant, tavern, or bar	25	15
Night club	12	17
Automobile	10	4
Private club	5	5
Other (includes military service for men)	19	10
Total	100	100

family members as companions. Drinking companions when first tight again reflect the sex differences already observed: for 64% of the men it was close friends of the same sex; for 64% of the women close friends in mixed company.

We have noted that 21% of the men students who drink and 35% of the women did not start until after they had entered college. Considering just these students, only 12% of the men and 28% of the women did their first drinking in college buildings. In many of the colleges drinking on campus was absolutely forbidden, the rule was rigidly enforced, and severe punishment imposed on violators. Under such conditions, it is not surprising to find most students drinking elsewhere.

Of all the students who had ever been tight, 75% of the men and 47% of the women reported it had happened before they entered college. Of those to whom it first happened while in college, it occurred in college buildings for 22% of the men and 15% of the women.

In considering drinking in college, it is important to realize the extent to which early drinking is a form of behavior associated with the family, and the relatively minor role the college plays as a place of first drinking. It is significant that first experiences of mild intoxication were overwhelmingly in the company of close friends, and that, again, the college did not figure prominently as the place where this initial intoxication was experienced.

Usual Student Drinking

The usual places of drinking according to type of beverage are shown for men and women in Table 57. It is clear that the three major types of beverage are ordinarily consumed in different settings. Most wine drinking takes place in homes, primarily own homes (74% for men and 82% for women); beer drinking usually occurs in restaurants, taverns, or bars (60% for men and 47% for women); for spirits the night club is the chief setting for both girls and boys, although a combination of one's own home and friend's home exceeds it for boys.

Striking as these differences are, the most interesting figures in the table are probably the very small percentages shown for fraternity and sorority houses as the usual setting for any type of drinking. These societies have often been pictured as drinking clubs or as encouraging drinking along with other undesirable forms of behavior. The negligible role reported for•them here casts considerable doubt on this stereotype.

Table 57: Usual Place of Drinking (in per cent)

Place	Men Beer	Wine	Spirits	Women Beer	Wine	Spirits
Own home	15	55	14	18	67	16
Home of a friend	9	19	18	13	15	14
College room	3	3	5	1	1	1
Fraternity or sorority house	3	1	3	6	—*	4
Restaurant, tavern, or bar	60	13	22	47	11	22
Night club	5	4	28	8	3	37
Private club	2	2	5	1	1	4
Other	3	3	5	6	2	2
Total	100	100	100	100	100	100

* <0.5%.

One approach to study of this question was to compare the incidence of drinking by members of fraternities and nonmembers. The comparison reveals that more students who belong to college societies drink and that they may drink a little oftener than nonmembers. However, more careful analysis reveals that this finding should by no means be construed as suggesting a direct correlation between fraternity membership and drinking. In the first place, there was considerable variation among the colleges. At several colleges society members and nonmembers showed no difference in drinking incidence. Furthermore, different societies on the same campus showed wide variation. There were several schools where the fraternities or sororities could be divided quite clearly into drinking and nondrinking societies, on the basis of the practice of a majority of their members. Nor was there consistency in the practices of members of certain national societies which had chapters on several of the campuses that were studied; in fact, there was substantial variation in the incidence of drinking between chapters. Although there are more drinkers among students who happen to belong to fraternities or sororities than among nonmembers, a direct association between society membership and drinking should not be construed. Membership in these societies is not at all homogeneous with respect to drinking. It varies from school to school, from society to society within a particular college, and from college to college within a particular national fraternity or sorority. The nonsociety population is not homogeneous either, and here too it is possible to identify clusters of users and of abstainers.

Our analysis leads us to the conclusion that the somewhat greater association of drinking with society membership is merely a reflection of other more significant factors. One of these may be the economic factor, the fact that there is more drinking among students of higher economic status. Although we do not have evidence that membership in fraternities or sororities is in general dependent on higher income, we do know that different societies tend to select their members from students of the same economic and social status. Still another important underlying factor in drinking and society membership is the behavior of one's close associates. We saw in Chapter 4 that students who drink usually reported that their close friends also drink. Close friends usually join the same societies. The rather complex picture of drinking and nondrinking fraternities and sororities suggests that drinking behavior does not stem from the society per se but rather from the current practices of the students who are associated in membership. This conclusion is supported by the existence of similar clusters of drinkers and nondrinkers among nonmembers.

We are led to the conclusion, after examining the matter from various angles, that the fraternity-nonfraternity dichotomy is not particularly meaningful with respect to the drinking customs of college students.

Let us now consider the influence of association with other students, by examining the incidence of drinking according to participation in extracurricular activities. It was noted in Chapter 5 that nearly half the male students who reported temporary abstention (going on the wagon) listed participation in sports as their reason for so doing. However, only 4% of the male abstainers reported that their main reason for abstaining was because alcohol interfered with their participation in sports. It is generally assumed, however, that athletes in training will abstain from alcohol.

Certainly abstention while in training is included in the list of rules issued by most athletic directors. With this in mind we divided extracurricular activities into athletic and nonathletic, and athletics (for men) into varsity and nonvarsity, on the assumption that varsity athletes would be more apt to refrain from alcohol because of the premium that membership on a varsity team would place on top physical fitness.

It should be stressed that we are considering here students who have at some time been users of alcoholic beverages in contrast to total abstainers. We are concerned merely with drinking or non-drinking according to types of extracurricular activity. The incidence of drinking among students according to various combinations of participation or nonparticipation in athletic and other activities appears in Table 58. Among men, with one exception, no

Table 58: Incidence of Drinking, according to Participation in Extracurricular Activities (in per cent)

Men	Students Who Are Users of Alcoholic Beverages
Varsity athletics plus other extracurricular activities	87
Varsity athletics but no other extracurricular activities	77
Nonvarsity athletics plus other extracurricular activities	76
Nonvarsity athletics but no other extracurricular activities	78
Nonathletic extracurricular activities only	76
No extracurricular activities	75
Women	
Athletic with or without other extracurricular activities	60
Nonathletic extracurricular activities only	56
No extracurricular activities	48

significant differences appear. The exception, contrary perhaps to expectation, is that group of students who are varsity athletes and also participate in other forms of outside activity: 87% of these drink as compared with 75 to 78% of all other male students.

Among women too, athletic participants included the greatest percentage of drinkers. Perhaps this is due to their greater degree of social activity. By and large the varsity athletes on a campus acquire considerable prestige. They may be in demand at various social functions because of the status associated with their athletic record. Those varsity athletes who also take part in other extracurricular activities have opportunities for still more association. Since drinking is a part of many social functions in our society, the probability of drinking increases with one's attendance.

Summary

From our survey of student drinking in terms of who, what, how much, when, where, with whom, and from what age, it becomes increasingly clear that drinking must be viewed as a complex social and cultural phenomenon. Alcohol, of course, may be described in chemical terms, and its ingestion has marked physiological and psychological effects. However, as the data we have presented chapter by chapter consistently reveal, the various aspects of drinking show clear correlations with ethnic and religious background, parental custom, family income, participation in religious and social activities, association, and the like.

The most frequently expressed views about college drinking or any category of drinking do not consider it as a cultural or social phenomenon. The usual explanations describe it in terms of free rational choice of the individual; of a desire to experience the anesthetic effects of alcohol or to satisfy a specific taste; a need to show off, act perversely, or defy authority; as a response to ubiquitous advertising; or, reflecting older theoretical traditions, as related to a biological factor (undefined) which "demands" alcohol consumption. These chapters clearly indicate that such explanations have at best a secondary significance: independently they are of small importance; within particular sociocultural settings their effects may or may not become more important. As obvious examples: rational choice, omnipresent advertising, or need to show off can hardly explain the clearly differentiated patterns of drinking vs. abstinence, of amounts consumed, or of type of beverage used which are disclosed for various ethnic or religious orientations or for those coming from families of different income levels.

No matter which of these sociocultural categories is selected, advertising, individual free choice, and need to show off are present in similar degree for all three. How can one explain not only drinking or not drinking but also patterned variations in type, amount, and frequency of drinking by means of a single, uniform cause? If advertising causes John to drink, what about Mary who does not? How is it that advertising seems to affect 80% of one religious group but only 30% of another? If rational individual choice or perversity explains the drinking of 70% of wealthier families, why does it affect only 40% of less wealthy parents or affect less wealthy Irish more strongly than less wealthy Negroes?

Stated in such terms, the traditional explanations of drinking given above become inconsequential. But inconsequential or not, they represent the prevailing philosophies of those who have educated young and old about drinking and alcohol, in formal and informal settings, in our society for at least a hundred years. They have been the major influence in legislation concerning alcohol and in enforcement. They have been the major type of explanation for church groups adhered to by millions. They have had a dominant influence in medical, health, and welfare groups.

Recorded data on the facts of drinking show that it is not only a sociocultural phenomenon but a complex one with many patterns. Furthermore, the patterns may appear to approach mutual exclusion, as in the comparisons of male and female drinking companionship and choice of beverage, or in the matter of drinking in childhood according to ethnic background, or in the presence or absence of drinking according to close friendship. This fact of multiple patterns of drinking is also in direct conflict with traditional concepts and related policies of schools, churches, governments, and other groups. Education, exhortation, legislation, and enforcement have all been couched in terms of drinking and not drinking. Except for the total abstainers, who happen to form a minority of the general population, actual behavior does not match these terms. As a necessary result, education, exhortation, legislation, and enforcement emanate with different meanings and are received with different interpretations. That confusion and conflict are associated with the use of alcoholic beverages in our society should prove no surprise once the distinction between popular concepts and actual behavior is perceived.

The facts about when and with whom our student segment of the population drinks raise highly significant questions about the morality of drinking. A large portion of our population has held drinking as such to be morally questionable if not clearly immoral. The number of students who report receiving specific warnings about alcohol (over 90%) and specific advice to abstain (almost half) easily substantiates this view. It is a truism that morality is defined, practiced, rewarded and, in its breach, punished most significantly in the family and in the friendship group. Yet it has been shown that drinking starts for the great majority in the home and family. This is almost completely the case for childhood drinking. For drinking beyond the childhood stage, first instances occurred above all in the boys' and girls' own homes and in the homes of friends. In drinking beyond the first instance, the usual companions were close friends and family. For the church, school, or government to act as if such behavior were immoral poses some very difficult conflicts indeed.

Recognition of drinking as a cultural and social phenomenon allows greater insight into drinking behavior. It also enables one to perceive more specifically the variations within the patterns, together with the related behavior commonly labeled "problem." Anomalies and pathologies always become more understandable and more susceptible of remedial action when the larger structures and processes, of which they form a painful and often dramatic part, are more carefully and exactly measured. For example, with increased knowledge of the blood and its circulation, understanding and control of certain specific diseases were increased. The chapters that follow will discuss some anomalous and problem behavior as well as some attitudes and beliefs related to drinking. These form special aspects of the whole constellation of drinking behavior. Viewed in the larger context they are more readily understood and become more susceptible of realistic control.

CHAPTER 10. *High, Tight, and Drunk*

We have stressed that one of the key problems in the use of alcoholic beverages by young people is intoxication. Although it is possible to make some crude predictions about the effect on behavior which a given concentration of alcohol in the blood (and therefore in the central nervous system) will produce in individuals, to measure the alcohol concentration in the blood of any individual at a given time requires precise equipment or specialized technical skill. Such a procedure was beyond the scope of the present study. Nor is it possible to make any accurate estimates of effect from data on quantity of alcohol consumption, for there is considerable variation in the behavioral effect which any given amount of alcohol will produce in different individuals. Blood alcohol concentration itself depends on such variable factors as weight, the content of the stomach at the time that alcohol is ingested, whether drinking is accompanied by eating, and the length of time consumed in ingesting a given amount of alcohol. Overt behavior under the influence of alcohol is also subject to certain psychological factors. For example, persons who are accustomed to specific physical sensations induced by alcohol may undergo them with little noticeable behavioral change, whereas persons experiencing the same sensations for the first time may react to the mere novelty in a way which exaggerates the alcohol effect or, more precisely, what the individuals think the effect should be.

In spite of these obstacles, it was felt important to achieve some estimate of the extent of influence which alcohol exerts on the behavior of college students who drink. Students who participated in the pretests were asked to describe some of their own sensations and behavior when drinking and to suggest terms which they felt were suitably descriptive of different levels of effect. From their responses and from supplementary discussions with these and other students, the terms high, tight, and drunk were selected as descriptive measures of effect which could be defined in terms of meaningful behavior. They were defined as follows:

High indicates a noticeable effect without going beyond socially acceptable behavior, e.g., increased gaiety, slight fuzziness of perception, drowsiness, and so on.

Tight suggests unsteadiness in ordinary physical activities, or noticeable aggressiveness, or oversolicitousness, or loss of control over social amenities or of verbal accuracy, or slight nausea.

Drunk suggests an overstepping of social expectancies (short of complete passing out), loss of control in ordinary physical activities, and inability to respond to reactions of others.

To complete the possible range of effect, the categories "no appreciable change in behavior or attitude" and "passed out" were also used.

In an initial attempt to measure effect from drinking, students were asked to estimate roughly the percentage of instances when one or more drinks produced no appreciable change in their behavior or attitude, and the percentage of such times when they became at least high. Table 59 shows that a fourth of the men who

Table 59: Percentage of Times Students Who Drink Report Becoming at Least High (in per cent)

Occasions	Students Who Drink	
	Men	Women
Under 10% or never	27	42
10 to 19%	21	20
20 to 49%	25	20
50 to 79%	18	13
80 to 100%	9	5
Total	100	100

drink and 42% of the women reported either that they had never been high or had been so less than 10% of the times they had consumed alcohol. Altogether, nearly half the men and almost two-thirds of the women experienced no appreciable change on at least eight out of ten drinking occasions. At the other end of the scale, 27% of the men and 18% of the women reported that they had become high, at least, on half or more of their drinking occasions. It appears then that a substantial segment of college students who drink have frequently experienced at least a level of effect from alcohol which results in gaiety, fuzziness, drowsiness, and the like, all within socially acceptable bounds. However, the majority of students report that on most occasions when they drink they are aware of no appreciable change in behavior. This is consistent with reports on quantities of alcoholic beverages consumed on specific drinking occasions. Chapter 8 showed that the majority of students usually consume what we defined as "smaller" amounts.

We turn now to the next level of effect, which we have called tight. Here are included definite unsteadiness or loss of control, possible aggressive behavior, and slight nausea. Students who drink were asked how many times in their lives they had been tight (Table 60). Nearly half the men and over four-fifths of the women

Table 60: Number of Times Student Drinkers Have Become Tight (in per cent)

| | Students Who Drink | |
Occasions	Men	Women
Never	20	51
1–5 times	25	32
6–15 times	18	9
16–50 times	17	4
51–100 times	5	—*
100 or more	4	—*
Have been tight, frequency not stated	11	4
Total	100	100

* <0.5%.

reported never or less than six times. Nine per cent of the men and less than 1% of the women reported they had been tight more than 50 times.

On the level labeled drunk, which includes various forms of extreme effect short of passing out, we find that 90% of the women

users and half of the men reported never having been drunk or
only once (Table 61).

Table 61: Number of Times Student Drinkers
Have Become Drunk (in per cent)

Occasions	Students Who Drink	
	Men	Women
Never	38	82
Once	13	8
2–5 times	27	8
6–10 times	8	1
11–20 times	5	— *
More than 20 times	5	— *
Have been drunk, frequency not stated	4	1
Total	100	100

* <0.5%.

The most advanced stage, passing out, is extremely rare by student report, occurring more than twice among only 1% of the
women users and among 9% of the male users (Table 62).

Table 62: Number of Times Student Drinkers
Have Passed Out (in per cent)

Occasions	Students Who Drink	
	Men	Women
Never	66	91
Once	16	7
Twice	8	1
3–5 times	6	1
6–10 times	2	— *
More than 10 times	1	— *
Have passed out, frequency not stated	1	— *
Total	100	100

* <0.3%.

Although the number of students who have been drunk more
than 5 times or passed out more than twice is small and the instances are spread over periods of years, these extreme forms of
drinking behavior should not be understated as a problem. Fortunately the students involved form a minority of the drinkers, al-

though their extreme behavior, because it is so painfully obvious
and dramatic, has often been included as a major part of the college drinking stereotype.

We have already seen in Chapter 8 that the quantity-frequency
index shows a positive relation to the number of times male students have been drunk and to the age at which they were first tight.
We have also seen in Chapter 9 that for 75% of the men and 47%
of the women who have been tight it occurred before entering college. Among those who had been tight, 10% of the men and 5%
of the women had been so before the age of 16; 41% of the men
and 37% of the women before the age of 18, and more than 80%
of each sex before the age of 20.

Does the weighting of students who first became tight while
quite young portend a pattern or merely reflect adolescent experimentation? Comparison of times tight by age when first tight supplies a clear answer. Of the male students who had first been tight
before the age of 16, 93% reported having been so more than five
times and 62% more than 25 times. Seventy-two per cent of those
first tight at ages 16 or 17 reported more than 5 times, 32% more
than 25 times. On the other hand, of those first tight at age 20
or later, 55% had been tight more than 5 times and only 23% more
than 25 times. Obviously, since the experience was more recent
for this group, they have not had as long to build up frequency.
But the findings clearly indicate that early intoxication cannot be
written off merely as childhood experimentation. The experience
was by no means an isolated one for the large majority of students
who first became tight before reaching their 18th birthday.

An examination of the frequency with which male students have
experienced the various levels of effect from alcohol fails to reveal
any significant variations according to family income. Students in
four categories of family income were compared according to a
number of criteria for measuring experience with different levels
of intoxication (Table 63). One can only be impressed by the extraordinary consistency of agreement in the incidence of each level
of intoxication among the various income groups. This is particularly interesting when it is recalled that frequency and quantity
of drinking were clearly related to family income.

When different religious and ethnic groups were compared

according to incidence of various levels of intoxication, it is note-worthy that the Jews and Italians consistently report less frequent intoxication than the other groups. These are the two cultural groups which more than all others use alcoholic beverages as an integral part of their way of life, wine having religious symbolism

Table 63: Levels of Intoxication, by Family Income (in per cent)

| | Male Students Who Drink | | | |
| | Family Income | | | |
Levels of Intoxication	Under $2,500	$2,500– $4,999	$5,000– $9,999	$10,000 and over
Never high or high on no more than 20% of drinking occasions	44	45	45	46
Never tight	23	18	23	17
Never drunk	33	34	42	34
Never passed out	67	68	69	64
High on at least 50% of drinking occasions	28	26	30	26
Tight more than 15 times	26	28	27	31
Drunk more than 5 times	20	16	17	18
Passed out more than once	19	14	20	18

or dietary importance for both. The comparatively low rates of intoxication among college students in these groups are all the more provocative in that these same groups stand out for their low rates of alcohol pathologies among adults (Table 64).

Relatively high rates of intoxication are to be observed among the Mormon male students who drink. We have already seen that Mormons as a group have a low incidence of users of alcohol, and we have related this to strong sanctions against drinking which are exerted by Mormon society. The fact that Mormon male students who do drink tend to experience the ill effects of alcohol with im-pressive frequency suggests the possible operation of a reaction against the prohibitive pressures of the church. By their mere drink-ing Mormon male students may in a sense be rebelling against these restrictions, and rebellion once turned loose often takes the form of extreme rather than mild reaction.

The above explanation can be examined further by comparing incidence of intoxication for all male students according to the advice which they have received against drinking. Table 65 shows that male students who drink and who reported receiving formal advice from religious leaders (but not from parents) to abstain show a higher incidence of being tight and drunk as well as frequency of both than do either the male student drinkers advised to abstain by parents or school authorities or those never advised to abstain. We recall the demonstration in Chapter 5 that the prob-

Table 64: Incidence of Intoxication, by Religion and Ethnic Background for Male Students Who Drink (in per cent)

	Those Who Have Ever			Tight	Drunk
	Been	Been	Passed	More Than	More Than
By Religion	Tight	Drunk	Out *	15 Times	5 Times
Mormon	88	74	40	28	25
Protestant	84	68	34	32	17
Catholic	73	56	33	24	15
Jewish	67	45	18	14	9
By Ethnic Group (excluding Jews and Mormons)					
British	83	66		29	20
German	81	61		30	19
Negro	79	55		16	9
American	77	60		24	14
Irish	76	57		24	16
Russian	73	57		22	14
Italian	70	49		16	12

* Not computed for ethnic groups.

Table 65: Frequency of Intoxication in Men, by Advice to Abstain (in per cent)

Male Students Who	Advice to Abstain			No advice
Drink Who Have Been	Parents	Church *	School †	to Abstain
Tight	80	89	72	80
Drunk	61	74	58	63
Tight more than 15 times	27	38	28	27
Drunk more than 5 times	18	25	17	16

* But not from parents.
† But not from parents or church.

ability that male students would be users as opposed to abstainers was greater for those who had been advised to abstain by church and by schools than for those advised by parents or not advised at all.

For women, however, the comparison of degrees and frequencies of intoxication with source of advice to abstain reveals quite the opposite pattern (Table 66). College women who drink although

Table 66: Frequency of Intoxication in Women, by Advice to Abstain (in per cent)

Female Students Who Drink Who Have Been	Advice to Abstain			No advice to Abstain
	Parents	Church *	School †	
Tight	58	40	52	52
Drunk	20	10	26	18
Tight more than 5 times	15	10	17	14

* But not from parents.
† But not from parents or church.

advised by the church to abstain are less likely to have been tight or drunk than all others. It will be recalled from Chapter 5 that the religious sanction against drinking was also relatively effective with women. This differential effectiveness is illustrated again by the fact that female users in the college category listed as "religious, 'dry' " have been tight or drunk considerably less often than all other women who use alcohol, while male drinkers in "religious, 'dry' " schools rate relatively high among all male drinkers in reported incidence of intoxication.

The effectiveness of religious sanctions against drinking for women, but not for men, may be explained in part by the differences shown in extent of participation in religious activities. In this study it was found that women in both the Protestant and Mormon groups participated in religious functions more frequently than men (half of these women attend church at least weekly, compared to a third of the men). This form of measurement is irrelevant for the Jewish group since negative sanctions on drinking are not found in this church. Nor can the measurement be meaningful for the Catholics from the information gathered by this survey because so many of the men were at parochial colleges where church attendance was compulsory, and no female parochial colleges which might balance this special effect were included in the study.

When only the men who were advised to abstain by their church are measured, 8% of the infrequent participants and 39% of the frequent participants abstained. Of the male infrequent participants who drank, 32% had been drunk more than five times; of the frequent participants only 19%. Among the women advised to abstain by their church, 69% of the regular churchgoers and only 29% of the others reported themselves as abstainers. From all these observations it is clear that extent of participation in a denomination is itself a significant factor, perhaps as important in its way as membership.

Striking consistency can be reported between frequency of intoxication and reasons for drinking. In Chapter 5 we saw that 47% of the male drinkers felt that "to get high" was an important reason for their drinking; 16% checked "to get drunk." Among the women 17% assigned importance to getting high and 1% to getting drunk. The reported frequency of intoxication is related in Table 67 to student ratings of "to get high" and "to get drunk" as reasons for drinking. For both men and women the percentage of users who assigned importance to getting high increases in direct proportion to the frequency of having been tight. Of those men who had never been tight only 10% rated getting high as important, compared with 37% of those who had been tight 1 to 5 times and so on up to 78% of those who had been tight more than 50 times. Women who rated "to get high" as of importance ranged from only 6% of those who had never been tight up to 45% of those who had been tight more than 15 times. Men who rated "to get drunk" as of importance included, curiously enough, 2% of those who had never been drunk, and 6% of those drunk only once in their lives, up to just over half of those who had been drunk more than 20 times.

We turn now from reasons for drinking to those questions which indicate a special stress put upon it: anticipatory drinking (before a party) and surreptitious drinking to get ahead of others.

Table 68 shows that only 6% of the anticipatory drinkers and 5% of the surreptitious drinkers claim never to have been tight, as compared with 27% of all other students. At the other extreme 40% of the anticipatory drinkers and 55% of those who sneak drinks have been tight more than 25 times compared with only 13% of all other students. Very similar comparisons are found when the respondents to these questions are compared according to times drunk. While a fourth as many students who sneak drinks have never been drunk as of those who answered both these questions in the negative, the relations are exactly reversed for being drunk more than 5 times.

Frequency of intoxication quite naturally is also closely correlated with the scale of social complications for men (Table 69).

Table 67: "To Get High" and "To Get Drunk" as Reasons of Some or Considerable Importance for Drinking, by Frequency of Intoxication (in per cent)

	Male Students
Frequency of Being Tight	*To Get High*
Never	10
1–5 times	37
6–15 times	52
16–25 times	58
25–50 times	75
More than 50 times	78

Frequency of Being Drunk	*To Get Drunk*
Never	2
Once	6
2–5 times	22
6–10 times	28
11–20 times	28
More than 20 times	52

	Female Students
Frequency of Being Tight	*To Get High*
Never	6
1–5 times	26
6–15 times	28
More than 15 times	45

Table 68: Frequency of Intoxication, by Measures of Special Stress on Drinking (in per cent)

| | Male Students Who Report That They | | |
Times Tight	drink before a party if not sure of getting any drinks or enough to drink	like to be one or two drinks ahead without others knowing it	do neither
Never	6	5	27
1–5 times	16	13	32
6–25 times	38	27	28
More than 25 times	40	55	13
Total	100	100	100
Times Drunk			
Never	20	12	45
Once	13	10	14
2–5 times	34	33	29
More than 5 times	33	45	12
Total	100	100	100

Table 69: Frequency of Intoxication, by Scale of Social Complications for Men (in per cent)

| | Social Complications Scale | | |
| | *0* | *1–2* | *3–4* |
Times Tight	None	Few	More Frequent
Never	30	5	0
1–5 times	30	23	8
6–25 times	27	39	29
More than 25 times	13	33	63
Total	100	100	100
Times Drunk			
Never	50	17	5
Once	14	11	9
2–5 times	26	44	23
More than 5 times	10	28	63
Total	100	100	100
Times Passed Out			
Never	78	53	33
Once	12	25	16
More than once	10	22	51
Total	100	100	100

Sixty-three per cent of the men with higher social complications ratings (3 or 4) have been tight more than 25 times, compared with 33% of those with a rating of 1 or 2 and only 13% of those rating zero. There are similar contrasts based on the frequency of being drunk and of passing out. These correlations are obviously to be expected, for the factors of complication which are included in our scale frequently involve some degree of intoxication. Had the relationship appeared less clear-cut, the validity of the complications scale as a useful measure would be subject to question.

We saw in Chapter 8 that the quantity and frequency of drinking by students bore a direct relationship to their attitude on the question "Should girls drink?" Students with high quantity-frequency indices, both men and women, were apt to allow girls freedom in drinking, while students with low Q-F indices were most likely to feel that girls should not drink at all or should restrict their drinking to beer and wine, with their low alcohol content. An attempt to determine whether a similar relationship existed between frequency of intoxication and this particular attitude failed to reveal any significant differences as between men who had never been tight or drunk and those who had experienced each level of effect seldom or more often.

Summary

A significant fact apparent from the data on being high, tight, and drunk is the small proportion of students experiencing the more advanced degrees of effect from alcohol, and the infrequency of such incidents for almost all. This again contrasts with the stereotype of college drinking as heavy, frequent, and often accompanied by drunkenness.

A more important conclusion, however, is suggested by the comparisons of students manifesting these extremes of drinking behavior according to the sociocultural factors used in earlier chapters: family income, religious and ethnic background, advice of parents. Certain significant differences in the incidence of drinking according to these criteria disappear or become reversed when the incidence of extreme drinking behavior is examined. This finding points strongly toward the following conclusion: cultural and social forces of a large, often impersonal nature play a highly significant role in the adoption or nonadoption of a behavior pattern; when and after a behavior pattern is adopted, cultural and social forces are still important in determining mode, frequency, and intensity of the individual manner of expressing the behavior, but individual and situational factors take on increasing significance; when extreme modes, intensities, and frequencies of action within a behavioral pattern are adopted, cultural and social forces of the large, often impersonal type play a very small role, and the individual and situational forces bulk large.

In terms of drinking behavior this conclusion suggests that differences in age, sex, ethnic origin, religious affiliation, wealth of parents and their example and attitude are extremely important factors in determining whether or not a given individual will or will not use alcohol. For example, one would predict on the basis of these findings that 9 out of 10 college students of Jewish extraction in the United States would use alcoholic beverages and that 8 out of 10 Mormon girls would not; that 8 out of 10 of those from families in high income brackets would drink and that 5 out of 10 from low income families would abstain—and so on. Similar predictions could be made about age, setting, and companions in relation to the first experience of drinking.

Once drinking had started, however, such high correlations and prediction value in terms of background cultural and social factors would tend to decrease. If the practice of drinking were extremely rigid in terms of what, when, where, how much, with whom and so on, then the decrease in the influence of such factors would be slight. If, as is more usually the case in this country, the patterns of drinking were rather flexible and poorly defined, one would expect the sociocultural correlations to drop more rapidly. If, for example, persons of German background drank only beer, in groups of men, after 6 P.M., never less than three or more than five glasses, with complete agreement as to the nutritive, religious, and social functions of drinking and similar reactions to it, then one would expect that predictions about the where, what, when, and so forth of drinking following inception of the practice could be made quite accurately according to age, ethnic origin, sex, and similar factors. But if the same young men had several varieties of behavior to choose from, all within the range of social expectancy, as to what, how much, how often, and with whom they drank, then predictability according to age, sex, ethnic origin, and so on would rapidly diminish.

For the individuals who, after beginning to drink, tended to adopt more extreme modes of the flexible pattern, it is clear that the background factors would have less and less prediction value. By definition, "extreme" implies proximity to the limits of social acceptance and expectancy, and automatically implies that the individual is consciously or unconsciously approaching rejection not only of preferential ways of expressing the behavior but also of prescribed limits. For drinking behavior this means that the extreme individuals will tend more and more to become like each other no matter what the differentials in the background. Individual and situational factors will tend to erase sociocultural influences.

This view certainly helps to explain some of the differences that appear from comparison of sociocultural factors with drinking or not drinking and from comparison of the same factors with absence or presence of extreme drinking. For nine groups of ethnic origin the percentage of males who drank was third highest among those of Italian origin and lowest among native white Americans (excluding Mormons and Jews). This order is strikingly changed when we consider the percentage of tight and drunk among drinkers of those groups. Those of Italian origin show the lowest percentage of men ever tight as well as of men ever drunk. Those of native white American origin are fourth highest in the percentage ranking of drinkers ever tight and third highest for those ever drunk. The orders have been almost reversed.

A similar situation exists for religious differences, as seen in the instance of Mormons and Jews. Ninety-four per cent of Jewish men drank, as against abstaining, and only 54% of Mormon men. However, for those male drinkers who drank to extremes the opposite relationship appears. As Table 64 showed, of the Jewish drinkers 67% had been tight, 45% had been drunk, and 18% had passed out. Of the Mormons who drink 88% had been tight, 74% drunk, and 40% had passed out.

These examples clearly show the effect of more and less rigidly defined patterns of drinking. The Jewish group presents an instance of well-defined drinking customs closely integrated with family and religious structures, with training or experience commencing in early childhood, and with uniform and strong disapproval of excessive effects. When the Jewish boy adopts the behavior pattern, even though he is living in the United States with its diffuse and confused drinking behavior and attitudes, the cultural and social factors pretty well maintain their strength. As is generally known, Jewish rates for alcoholism and for arrest for drunkenness are far lower than for any other comparable category of persons. Individual and situational anomalies—as varied for Jewish individuals as for individuals of any other group—cannot produce such extreme manifestations within the realm of their drinking behavior as is possible within the less well-defined drinking patterns of other cultural groups.

Men and women of Italian origin do not possess drinking customs as well defined or as unaffected by the dominant host culture as the customs of those of Jewish extraction. Nevertheless, compared to the native white, non-Jewish parts of our society, their tradition is fairly clear-cut, in spite of being at present in a stage of transition. Their drinking custom is not integrated with religion as is the Jewish custom; nor does there appear to be as strong disapproval of medium effects of drinking. However, the general use of wine, the association of meals with drinking, the dominance of family and home routines in the drinking picture, and the training and experience in drinking from an early age all mark the Italian custom as better defined and more socially powerful than the drinking folkways of the native white group. Individual variation and adoption of extremes within the behavior would be less than average, but more prevalent than among the group of Jewish origin.

The Mormon group obviously is found at the opposite pole. If drinking behavior is adopted, variation must be the rule since there is no norm. Extremes are likely since the behavior itself represents rejection of social rules. The models for behavior are either members of other groups or dissident members of their own group. Individual and situational factors cannot be restrained by sociocultural definitions of what is proper for drinking since such definitions do not exist. It is not surprising, then, to find that among those who drink 14% of the Jewish men were tight more than 15 times, 16% of the Italians, 24% of the white, non-Jewish, non-Mormon Americans, and 28% of the Mormons; 9% of the Jewish men were drunk more than 5 times, 12% of the Italians, 14% of the white, non-Jewish, non-Mormon Americans, and 25% of the Mormons.

This conception of the differential effect shown by sociocultural forces on the one hand and individual and situational forces on the other is also substantiated by comparison of extreme behavior and extreme statements of the justification or purpose of drinking. Sociocultural forces are even more influential on statements explaining behavior, or rationalizations, than they are on behavior itself, a fact that has been remarked upon for more than two thousand years: what people *say* is more likely to approach their cultural preferences or ideals than what they do. Getting high would rarely be held a virtue or a proper purpose by a religious, ethnic, or similar group. Getting drunk would be frowned on by almost any such group. Yet over three-quarters of those tight 25 times or more rated getting high as an important reason for drinking, and over half of those who were drunk more than 20 times reported getting drunk as an important reason. It is clear that in these cases individual responses have broken away from the sociocultural forces in emphatic fashion.

We shall consider later the significance that this idea of differential forces operating on the moderate drinkers and the extreme drinkers has for attempts to change group behavior, to meet the problem of the alcoholic, and to increase understanding of conflicting attitudes about alcohol.

CHAPTER 11. *The Veteran in College*

Since our survey was conducted in the years 1949 through 1951, a sizable proportion of veterans was naturally included among the participants. Actually there were proportionately a good many more veterans at the colleges which were visited in 1949 than at those visited later in the period, for the influx of veterans reached our colleges during the late 1940's and its peak had decidedly passed by 1950. Among all the participants in the study 44% of the men and 2% of the women had seen service in the armed forces or in such other wartime services as the merchant marine or the Red Cross Field Service. Actually the last two categories were of minor numerical importance, but all are classified as veterans for present purposes.

The adjustment problems of veterans in college have been the subject of much speculation and a good deal of investigation.[1] Our own study would be obviously inadequate if we failed to consider possible differences in drinking pattern and attitude between those students who had been subjected to the stresses of wartime services and those who had not. Because of the small number of women veterans we shall restrict our consideration to men.

There are many factors which would lead to a logical supposition that veterans would be more apt than nonveterans to be drinkers and that because of their experience in the armed forces they would be more likely to have taken part in intensive drinking. It might be argued that veterans have had both greater opportunity and

1. For a comprehensive and detailed analysis of this subject see Norman Frederiksen and W. B. Schrader, *Adjustment in College* (Educational Testing Service, Princeton, 1951).

greater incentive for drinking. Entrance into the armed forces involves separation from parents and removal of parental controls. Situations present themselves in which there are strong sanctions for drinking. Entering the services also means an abrupt change from an environment characterized by emphasis on individual initiative and consideration for the individual to one calling for almost complete subordinacy of the individual to the organization and the cause for which it exists.

The newness, rigidity, discipline, monotony, and pervasive character of military life, affecting every attitude and action every hour of every day, may well have enhanced the meaning of any recreation, especially away from the military setting. In addition to this increased significance of any off-duty activity for the military man, alcohol itself allows temporary escape from unpleasant reality, and the expression of degrees of individuality and aggression ordinarily suppressed. Furthermore, drinking is generally held to enliven celebrations, and many young people think it a sign of sophistication and virility; these two attitudes may present problems to young men many of whom are away from home and neighborhood for the first time. A number of off-duty situations can readily be interpreted as "demanding" drinking.

Veterans in college also manifest certain basic characteristics which differentiate them significantly from the nonveteran. One of these is family income. The G.I. Bill of Rights put a college education within the reach of many young people who without it would not have gone beyond high school. A comparison of veterans and nonveterans by family income (Table 70) shows that two-thirds of the veterans as compared with less than half (44%)

Table 70: Family Income, by Veteran Status for Men (in per cent)

Family Income	Nonveterans	Veterans
Under $2,500	14	23
$2,500–$4,999	30	43
$5,000–$9,999	29	24
$10,000 and over	27	10
Total	100	100

of other students had a family income of less than $5,000; only
10% of the veterans compared with 27% of all others reported
family incomes of $10,000 or more. Of course it must be remem-
bered that subsistence allotments to veterans provided some with
much more pocket money than they would normally have had. We
have already seen that students from high income families show
a higher incidence of drinking and somewhat higher quantity-
frequency indices than those from low income families. However,
we have seen no apparent relationship between income and choice
of beverage or incidence of intoxication.

A second characteristic of veterans in college which differ-
entiates them sharply from nonveterans is their age: the fact that
they are considerably older than students who entered college
directly from high school or did not have their college years interrupted. We see in Table 71 that 35% of the nonveterans are under
19, but none of the veterans; that only 7% of the nonveterans are

*Table 71: Age, by Veteran Sta-
tus for Men (in per cent)*

Age	Nonveteran	Veteran
18 or below	35	0
19–21	58	18
22 or above	7	82
Total	100	100

22 or above, but 82% of the veterans. The data on quantity and
frequency, it will be recalled, show a decided peak in drinking at
about 21, with a downward trend in consumption after that age.
Thus, while their service experience might be assumed to have influenced veterans toward drinking, their being older and from
somewhat lower economic background than nonveterans may
weigh slightly in the other direction.

Considering merely the factor of drinking or abstaining, we
find in Table 72 that the college veteran population contained
just a slightly higher incidence of users of alcoholic beverages than
the nonveterans: 83% as against 76%. There are no great differences in choice of beverage (Table 73). No significant differences
appear between veteran and nonveteran users compared accord-

THE VETERAN IN COLLEGE

ing to the quantity-frequency index (Table 74). For the year just preceding participation in the survey, at least, veterans at college do not appear to have consumed alcoholic beverages more fre-

Table 72: Incidence of Drinking, by Veteran Status (in
per cent)

	Nonveterans	Veterans
Abstainers	24	17
Users	76	83
Total	100	100

Table 73: Type of Beverage
Most Frequently Used, by
Veteran Status (in per cent)

	Students Who Drink	
	Nonveteran	Veteran
Beer	68	73
Wine	6	4
Spirits	26	23
Total	100	100

quently or in greater amounts than nonveterans. Veterans who drink were also asked whether they drink more or less often than they did in service. It is significant to find that 38% reported drinking just as often, 12% said more often in college, and just 50% said that they drink less frequently in college. Furthermore, as might be expected, the students drinking more frequently in col-

Table 74: Quantity-Frequency Index, by Veteran Status (in per cent)

Quantity-Frequency Index	Students Who Drink	
	Nonveterans	Veterans
1	26	21
2	15	17
3	14	20
4	28	24
5	17	18
Total	100	100

lege than in service are most heavily weighted in the higher quantity-frequency index scores. Fifty-nine per cent of these students had a Q-F index of 4 or 5, as compared with 38% of those who drink less often in college and 35% of those who reported that they drink as often as they did in the service. Thus, while the veteran population in college appears to drink about as much and as often as the nonveteran college group, half of the veterans report that they drank more often while they were in service.

At this point certain distinctions between life in military service and at college deserve comment. Students in college are working for their personal advancement, while most men in the service are working in a situation which is removed from their normal course of life. After five or six days of classes, the student probably does not feel the urge to go out and drink as much as the serviceman who goes off for a week-end pass. In college there is continuity of custom; in the service the custom (of recreation) is a catch-as-catch-can pastime, since the dictates of wartime military requirements do not permit settled schedules. In the service the veteran had less of an opportunity to choose his companions than in college, and far less of an opportunity to choose his particular kind of recreation.

Table 75 compares veterans with nonveterans on the basis of frequency of having been tight or drunk or having passed out.

Table 75: Frequency of Intoxication, by Veteran Status (in per cent)

| | Students Who Drink | |
	Nonveterans	Veterans
Never tight	27	12
Never drunk	46	25
Never passed out	74	60
Tight more than 50 times	3	13
Drunk more than 10 times	5	15
Passed out more than twice	4	11

Here we see the veterans outstripping the nonveterans. Veterans who have been tight more than 50 times exceed nonveterans by 4 to 1, and those who have been drunk more than ten times or

passed out more than twice exceed the nonveterans by 3 to 1. The
fact that veterans at college have had more experience of intoxication than other college students is clear. But we have still to determine whether this is associated with their veteran status or
merely reflects the fact that they are on the average several years
older and have had more time to accumulate these experiences.

First we shall compare all veterans with all nonveterans according to several further criteria of drinking. The two groups
showed almost identical distribution of responses to the question
on the extent to which girls of college age should drink. Responses
on anticipatory drinking and sneaking of drinks are shown in
Table 76, and a comparison according to the social complications
scale appears in Table 77. In both Tables 76 and 77 veterans show

*Table 76: Measures of Special Stress on Drinking, by
Veteran Status (in per cent)*

	Students Who Report That They		
	drink before a party if not sure of getting any drinks or enough to drink	like to be one or two drinks ahead without the others knowing it	do neither
Nonveterans	28	10	70
Veterans	28	12	62

*Table 77: Social Complications Scale, by Veteran
Status (in per cent)*

	Students Who Drink	
Scale	Nonveterans	Veterans
0 (no complications)	70	62
1–2 (few complications)	25	30
3–4 (more frequent complications)	5	8
Total	100	100

slightly greater positive weightings than nonveterans. Negative
responses to both measures of special stress on drinking were recorded by 70% of the nonveterans and 62% of the veterans. Zero,
or no complications, curiously enough was recorded also by just
70% of the nonveterans and 62% of the veterans. In the case of the
complications from drinking, the lifetime cumulative experience

is recorded, so in this instance differences could easily be accounted for by age alone. In fact, considering the discrepancy in age between the veterans and other students, a considerably greater difference in incidence of social complications might well have been expected.

If the stresses and exigencies of military service have affected the drinking patterns of veterans, differences might be expected to appear in the values they place on their drinking when compared with nonveterans. We compared the two groups on the basis of the importance they assign to various reasons for drinking. In Table 78 twelve reasons for drinking are listed, together with the percentages of veterans and nonveterans who ascribed importance to

Table 78: Reasons for Drinking, by Veteran Status (in per cent)

	Users Assigning Some or Considerable Importance to Each Reason		Percentage Difference Veterans Compared to Nonveterans
	Nonveterans	Veterans	
To get along better on dates	37	30	− 7
To relieve fatigue or tension	48	60	+12
To be gay	62	63	+ 1
To relieve illness or physical discomfort	24	26	+ 2
To comply with custom	65	62	− 3
Because of enjoyment of taste	73	71	− 2
In order not to be shy	25	26	+ 1
As an aid in meeting crises	9	10	+ 1
For a sense of well-being	18	22	+ 4
As an aid in forgetting disappointments	26	25	− 1
To get high	47	46	− 1
To get drunk	16	15	− 1

each. We are confronted here with remarkable similarity. On exactly half of the items there is a difference of merely one percentage point. The difference exceeds 5 points on only two items.

Nonveterans were a little more apt to feel that drinking helped them get along better on dates, while veterans were more likely to value it as a means of relieving fatigue or tension. In the last instance, at least, there is plausible explanation in the veterans' past experience. Most of them have been exposed to degrees of fatigue and tension which are not comparable to anything the average non-veteran has known.

The picture that has appeared so far shows the drinking patterns of veterans in college, far from being unlike those of nonveteran students, to be strikingly similar. For the most part the only differences have been in criteria which measured cumulative experience. We must still ascertain to what extent cumulative differences (frequency of intoxication and complications) may be related to differences in age rather than to the experience of military service. Also, since we have seen that nonveterans are somewhat more heavily weighted with the economically well-to-do, we want to consider what effect the economic factor may have had as an equalizer that might have acted to conceal a greater incidence of drinking among veterans if compared with nonveterans of comparable family income. Other factors which have been found associated in one way or another with particular drinking traits should also be accounted for.

In order to measure the effect of other factors on apparent veteran-nonveteran differences a small sample of matched veterans and nonveterans was selected from the participants in the study, paired according to age, race, religion, college year, family income, and the type of college they were attending. The matched pairs were then compared according to the following items of drinking: the quantity-frequency profile (with abstainers assigned the index zero), several attitudes (to be considered in Chapter 13); the number of times tight, drunk, and passed out; the relative strength (in terms of alcohol content) of the type of beverage preferred and that most frequently used; the amount consumed of the type of beverage most frequently used; frequency of drinking in mixed company; attitude to drunkenness; and perceived relationship between drinking and sexual behavior. The intricacies of operation involved in this comparison made it necessary to restrict our analysis to a relatively small group, although we would have preferred a more exhaustive analysis.[2] In no instance were signifi-

2. Within the 10% sample of students 38 matched pairs were found. The total selection should therefore yield about 380 pairs based on the 6 criteria of comparison.

cant differences between veterans and nonveterans found when
age, income, and the other factors enumerated above were held
constant. Our analysis leads to the conclusion that college drinking
patterns of veterans and nonveterans show remarkable similarity.
Differences that do appear are largely in factors which measure
cumulative experience, and disappear when age and other factors
are held constant. In the case of veterans, and probably for nonveterans of comparable age, college education has been delayed
or interrupted, and both groups share in common the fact of some
type of interim experience. There is no evidence in the drinking
histories to suggest that this interim experience involved more or
less drinking, whether military or nonmilitary.

A further question should be raised regarding drinking and the
veteran: how many of the veterans started to drink while in service, and to what extent if any does their present drinking differ
from that of veterans who had been introduced to drinking before
their military experience? Table 79 shows that three-fourths of

Table 79: Veterans' Experience of Drinking,
(in per cent)

	Veterans Who Are Users	Veterans Who Have Been Tight
	First Drink	First Tight
Before service	76	53
During service	22	43
After service	2	4
Total	100	100

the veterans who are users started their drinking before entering
military service, 22% started while in service, and only 2% did
not start until afterward. Just over half of the veterans who have
been tight (and 88% of all veteran users have been tight) first
experienced it before entering service, 43% first while in service,
and only 4% afterward. Thus less than a fourth of the veteran
users started drinking while in service; less than half of those who
have been tight first experienced it while in service.

Such relationship between initiation to drinking in service and
later drinking patterns as appears is one of less drinking in college.

Of the veterans who first drank before service 44% have a high quantity-frequency index of 4 or 5, as compared with only 32% of those who started drinking in service. Of the veterans who first became tight before military service 49% have a Q-F rating of 4 or 5, compared with 38% of those who first became intoxicated while in service.

Summary

The findings of the present chapter certainly do not support a theory that the stresses, restrictions, and sanctions of military service have left any distinctive mark on the drinking patterns of veterans in college. The only significant differences in the drinking behavior of veterans compared with nonveterans were found in factors which measured cumulative behavior; and these tended to disappear for subjects of equal age. Students who first drank or first became tight while in service actually tend to drink a little less extensively than veterans whose initial experiences preceded service. Therefore, allowing for individual exceptions, we must reject any notion that drinking practices initiated in service have led to particularly extensive or intensive drinking patterns in veterans.

CHAPTER 12. *The Potential Problem Drinker*

It is rare for the subject of drinking to be discussed without some reference to alcoholism. Among the many and varied problems connected with alcohol the hardships and heartaches often associated with chronic uncontrolled drinking are likely to command the greatest share of public attention. Not many years ago alcoholism was one of the unmentionable disorders and like tuberculosis and cancer was never referred to in polite society. Today, however, the skeleton is no longer kept hidden in the closet. Scientific effort is at last being directed toward discovering the causes of alcoholism and effective methods of rehabilitation for the alcoholic. Alcoholism has become a commonplace topic for magazine articles and for meetings of church groups and civic organizations. A movement in public health education is gradually creating better understanding and sympathy for the alcoholic among the general public. Special provisions for dealing with alcoholism as a public health problem have been made by the legislatures of 41 states and by several municipalities.

Fortunately, alcoholism is not a significant problem in the college population. There are comparatively few persistent problem drinkers among the age group 17 through 23. Alcoholism is a progressive disorder which, particularly in males, usually takes from 10 to 20 years to develop. To be sure, there are incidents of problem drinking among college students, and there are individuals whose drinking patterns display certain warning signs which may suggest that they are potential problem drinkers. But it is important to differentiate between incidental problem drinking and that which may be repetitive and patterned. It is the latter with which this chapter is concerned.

We still know very little about the causes of alcoholism. The majority of investigators agree that psychological and environmental factors are of prime importance, although it is possible that some as yet undefined physiological factors may be involved. While specific causes have not been discovered, studies of alcoholics made in retrospect have identified certain types of behavior which seem characteristic of incipient problem drinking. In the present chapter we shall consider some experiences which are often characteristic of the potential problem drinker, and examine the extent to which they were reported by students in our study.

Social Complications

One group of questions which sheds some light on potential problem drinking concerns drinking behavior that inflicts injury or marked inconvenience on oneself or others. Students were asked whether drinking had ever interfered with their preparation for classes or examinations, caused them to lose close friends or damaged friendships, made them miss appointments or lose a job, resulted in accident, injury, or arrest, or brought them before college authorities.

In analyzing the responses to these questions it was possible to employ a device known as scaling.[1] The scalable characteristic was that of social complications associated with drinking. At the lowest point on the social complications scale (most likely to occur without implying occurrence of other items) were the questions about failure to meet academic or social obligations (drinking had at some time interfered with preparation for classes or examinations or resulted in missing an appointment). At the second scale position were the questions on loss of friends or damage to friendships attributed to drinking. Next came drinking which had caused ac-

1. In scale analysis the items making up the scale are so related that a positive response to one item implies positive responses on certain other items. The items in a scale represent a variety of magnitudes of some characteristic common to them all. See papers by Louis Guttman in *Measurement and Prediction, Studies in Social Psychology in World War II*, Vol. *4*, by Samuel A. Stouffer et al. (Princeton University Press, 1950).

cident or injury. Last came the questions about formal punishment or discipline because of drinking (loss of a job, arrest, or coming before college authorities). The scale types of our social complications scale can be illustrated as follows: [2]

Scale Type	Item A (Failure to Meet Obligations)	Item B (Damage to Friendships)	Item C (Accident or Injury)	Item D (Formal Punishment or Discipline)
0 (no complications)	—	—	—	—
1	+	—	—	—
2	+	+	—	—
3	+	+	+	—
4	+	+	+	+

The social complications scale allows us to draw conclusions such as the following: Students who have at any time suffered loss of a job or arrest or discipline by college authorities because of drinking have probably also at some time or other sustained an accident or injury while drinking, damaged their friendships, and failed to meet some social or academic obligations. Students for whom drinking has never entailed damage to friendships have probably never suffered injury or formal punishment for drinking but may have failed to meet obligations. Students for whom drinking has entailed damage of friendship may or may not ever have suffered injury or formal punishment but have very probably at some time failed to meet obligations.

The distribution of students who drink, according to the social complications scale, is shown in Table 80. Two-thirds of the men and 85% of the women reported no complications at all and are therefore classified as scale type zero. Seventeen per cent of the men and 8% of the women are scale type 1, indicating that they have

2. Irregular scale responses are assigned to the scale pattern which they fit with a minimum of error. For example the response + — + + would be assigned to scale type 4. A criterion for measuring the reliability of the scale is the frequency of assignment of nonscale patterns to a scale type. An acceptable scale is one in which errors of placement necessitated by assigning nonscale patterns to a scale type constitute no more than 10% of the total placements. Such a scale is said to have a 0.90 coefficient of reproducibility. The social complications scale in this study has a 0.97 coefficient of reproducibility.

at one time or another missed social obligations because of drink-ing but have suffered no other types of complication. Eleven per cent of the men and 6% of the women are scale type 2 and have also at some time or other suffered damage to a friendship which

Table 80: Students Who Drink, by
Social Complications Scale (in
per cent)

Scale Type	Students Who Drink	
	Men	Women
0 (no complications)	66	85
1	17	8
2	11	6
3	4	1 *
4	2	0
Total	100	100

* Actually <0.7%.

they attribute to drinking. Scale types 3 and 4 contain virtually no women, but 6% of the male drinkers report an accident or injury associated with drinking, in addition to the above complications, and 2% also report formal punishment or discipline.

The usefulness of a measure like our social complications scale is not limited to determining a meaningful relationship between various items of information. It also serves as an index for com-paring with other aspects of behavior the whole complex of be-havioral items which it covers. We have already seen in Chapter 8 a rather striking correlation between the social complications scale and the quantity and frequency of drinking. In Chapter 10 we saw that men with high complications scale ratings tended to be frequently intoxicated. The scale was also considered in relation to the basic identifying factors of age, income, and religion. Since the probability of experiencing one of the complications increases cumulatively with advancing age, it was expected that the scale would show a direct correlation to age. However, significant dif-ferences did not appear for either men or women beyond the age of 18. For both sexes, those 18 or less showed lower complications scale ratings than all older students.

Among women the probability of experiencing complications

decreased as family income increased (Table 81). Women with complications scale values of 1 through 4 comprised from 25% of the users with family incomes under $2,500 down to only 10% of those with family incomes of $10,000 or more. Among men, a

Table 81: Social Complications Scale, by Family Income (in per cent)

Social Complications Scale	Students Who Use Alcoholic Beverages			
	Family Income			
	Under $2,500	$2,500–$4,999	$5,000–$9,999	$10,000 and over
Men				
0	65	65	74	58
1–4	35	35	26	42
Total	100	100	100	100
Women				
0	75	81	86	90
1–4	25	19	14	10
Total	100	100	100	100

somewhat different relationship between income and complications scale appeared. The income bracket $5,000 to $9,999 contained the smallest percentage of male users who had experienced any of the complications (26%). The top income group ($10,000 or more) had the highest incidence of some complications (42%) while the two lower income brackets each contained 35% with some complications scale rating.

Students of different religions also displayed rather sharp differences in incidence of social complications, as shown in Table 82. Among men who are users complications have been experienced by only 20% of the Jewish students, by about a third of the Protestants and Catholics, and by 42% of the Mormons. Sharper distinctions in the same direction are seen among women users, ranging from only 2% of the Jews up to 41% of the Mormons. The low incidence of complications reported by Jewish students and the equally high incidence among Mormons can be explained in part in terms of the drinking sanctions of these two groups and the nature of certain complications scale components. It will be recalled that loss of friends and damage to friendships were items in-

cluded in the scale. In view of the strong Mormon sanctions against
the use of alcoholic beverages, it is readily conceivable that students who drink even in moderation would risk losing the respect
of their Mormon friends. As we have seen in Chapter 4, nearly half

Table 82: Social Complications Scale, by Religion (in
per cent)

Social Complications Scale	Students Who Are Users of Alcoholic Beverages			
Men	Catholic	Jewish	Mormon	Protestant
0	65	80	58	66
1–4	35	20	42	34
Total	100	100	100	100
Women				
0	89	98	59	84
1–4	11	2	41	16
Total	100	100	100	100

the Mormon men and three-fourths of the women are abstainers.
Also, most of the Mormon students were attending colleges with
predominantly Mormon enrollment, and at these schools even
slight drinking might subject a student to the discipline of college
authorities. The high complications ratings for Mormons do not
seem to be a result of frequent or extensive drinking; Chapter 8
showed both men and women Mormon students who drink to
have lower quantity-frequency indices than students of other
religions. But Mormon male students who drink did report fairly
frequent intoxication (Chapter 10). Intoxication and complications together suggest a reaction pattern. Those students who break
away from restrictions of their religious sanctions seem inclined
to react in a more emphatic, perhaps rebellious, manner than students whose drinking involves less rejection of their group. Jewish
students come from a background which sanctions moderate drinking. Like the Mormons they did not show high quantity-frequency
ratings, and unlike the Mormons they reported comparatively
infrequent experience of the various levels of intoxication. Nearly
all the Jewish friends of Jewish students also drink; and many of
the Jewish students were attending colleges which condoned moderate drinking by students. Furthermore, the sanctions of the Jew-

ish group, while encouraging appropriate drinking, look with disfavor upon any behavior which reflects unfavorably upon the individual or the group. It is not moderate drinking but that leading to complications which involves rejection of members of their group by Jewish students; this behavior is avoided by the majority. Findings on social complications according to religious affiliation are obviously consistent with those on intoxication and tend to support the type of explanation offered in Chapter 10.

In addition to the items which have been grouped in the social complications scale, several additional questions were asked in an effort to identify the potential problem drinker.

Special Stress on Drinking

Those factors were considered which suggest a tendency to place greater than normal stress on the importance of drinking. Anticipatory and surreptitious drinking have been considered in this connection in previous chapters, with the finding that students who drink before going to a party and students who like to be one or two drinks ahead of others tend to drink more frequently and in larger amounts than others and have more often experienced various levels of intoxication. Altogether, 26% of the male users and 9% of the women reported sometimes drinking in anticipation of not getting enough; 10% of the men and 2% of the women indicated that they sometimes drink surreptitiously. Both these kinds of behavior have been reported [3] as common to the early phases of problem drinking, although both (particularly anticipatory drinking) are occasionally shown by persons who would be designated as normal drinkers.

Another attempt to measure the importance students attached to drinking was made by seeking reactions to the hypothetical party or gathering where it might have been expected that alcoholic beverages would be served but they were not. Thirty-six per cent of the male drinkers and 23% of the women indicated that under such circumstances they would "sometimes feel that a party is a flop." Twenty-seven per cent of the men and 14% of the women

3. E. M. Jellinek, *The Phases of Alcohol Addiction*. World Health Organization, Tech. Rep. Ser. No. 48, August 1952. Also in *Quarterly Journal of Studies on Alcohol, 13* (December 1952), 673–684.

would "sometimes make comments" about the absence of drinks. However, only 8% of the men and 2% of the women said they would "probably refuse a future invitation." Just half the men and 69% of the women answered all three questions in the negative, which suggests that they attached no particular importance to whether alcohol is served at such functions or not.

As still another indication of special emphasis on the importance of drinking, students were asked whether the cost of liquor had ever caused them to forego other things. Eleven per cent of the male users and only 2% of the women reported that this had happened. Four per cent of the men and no women reported that on more than 5 occasions they had been short of money because of drinking. Women, of course, doing most of their drinking in mixed company, are likely to be treated by their male companions. It was found that students who reported being short of cash tended to have higher family incomes than any of the other students. This was also true, we remember, of students who reported that they abstain because they cannot afford to drink; the economic factor failed to explain why some students reported using beer (which is cheaper) although they preferred spirits (which are more expensive). Again we have evidence that feeling poor is relative to many factors other than actual income. The question about foregoing other things because of the cost of liquor was related to the extent of drinking and to social complications; 66% of the males who reported foregoing other things had high quantity-frequency indices (4 or 5) compared with only 41% of the other users; 72% of them had experienced social complications, as against 29% of the other users.

Additional Warning Signs

Next we shall consider four questions which, while not suggesting special stress on the importance of drinking, have definitely been identified as common warning signs of potential problem drinking.[4] These include a form of temporary amnesia known as the "blackout," becoming drunk when alone, drinking before or instead of breakfast, and participating when drinking in aggressive or wantonly destructive behavior.

4. Jellinek, *The Phases of Alcohol Addiction.*

The blackout is a term which alcoholics have adopted from aviation, where it is commonly used to refer to anoxemia. Students were asked whether they had ever awakened after a party or a drinking spree with no idea where they had been or what they had done after a certain point, although they had not passed out. This amnesia is not associated with a loss of consciousness. In fact, the drinker may never even have displayed any of the usual signs of intoxication. He may have carried on conversations and complicated activities without having any recollection of it the next day. Blackouts may happen, though rarely, to average drinkers who consume rather large amounts in a state of physical or emotional exhaustion. They have been reported quite frequently by alcoholics as an occurrence which antedated other positive signs of problem drinking. Although comparatively little is known about this phenomenon (it may be associated with malutilization of oxygen), its occurrence, particularly after taking only medium amounts of alcohol, is believed to be characteristic of the prospective alcohol addict. Eighteen per cent of the male student users and 5% of the women reported having experienced it. Only 1% of the women had blacked out more than once; 9% of the men had had only one blackout, and 1% reported more than 5.

Becoming intoxicated when alone is also identified as a warning sign of possible deviant drinking behavior. Drinking is primarily a social custom, and most people usually drink in company. While lone drinking is not uncommon among men (52% of the men and 4% of the women in our study reported that they had at some time or other had one or more drinks alone), drinking to the point of extreme intoxication when alone is considered pathological. Thirteen per cent of the male users and 3% of the women reported that they had become drunk when alone. This had occurred more than twice for 6% of the men and 1% of the women.

Another form of behavior quite common in the pathological drinker is early morning drinking, especially before or instead of breakfast. Positive responses to the question "Have you had one or more drinks before breakfast or instead of breakfast?" were recorded by 16% of the men and 7% of the women; 10% of the men and 3% of the women reported doing it more than twice.

Drinking which had led to aggressive, wantonly destructive, or malicious behavior (such as picking fights without provocation, vicious slander, damaging parked cars or other property, playing dangerous jokes on others) was reported by 11% of the men and less than 1% of the women. For 7% of the men it had occurred more than twice.

Students who had experienced any one of these four warning signs were found to be more extensive drinkers than those who had not (Table 83), and were much more apt to have experienced social complications (Table 84). All four forms of behavior together suggest either an abnormal reaction to or desire for alcohol or an asocial drinking pattern.

Table 83: Four Warning Signs, by Male Quantity-Frequency Index (in per cent)

Student Drinkers Who Have Ever Experienced		Quantity-Frequency Index			
		1	*2–3*	*4–5*	*Total*
Blackout	Yes	13	25	62	100
	No	26	34	40	100
Becoming drunk alone	Yes	7	30	63	100
	No	26	33	41	100
Drinking before or instead of breakfast	Yes	4	26	70	100
	No	27	34	39	100
Aggressive behavior, etc., when drinking	Yes	0	27	73	100
	No	26	33	41	100

Table 84: Four Warning Signs, by Male Social Complications Scale (in per cent)

Student Drinkers Who Have Ever Experienced		Social Complications Scale			
		0	*1–2*	*3–4*	*Total*
Blackout	Yes	46	33	21	100
	No	71	26	3	100
Becoming drunk alone	Yes	34	44	22	100
	No	72	24	4	100
Drinking before or instead of breakfast	Yes	34	44	22	100
	No	87	11	2	100
Aggressive behavior, etc., when drinking	Yes	30	40	30	100
	No	70	26	4	100

It should be stressed that the majority of the students who reported any of these four warning signs had experienced only one or two incidents. Two-thirds of the male drinkers had never experienced any of the warning signs, 22% reported only one of the four phenomena, 8% reported two, and 5% reported three or four; 94% of the female drinkers had never experienced any of these warning signs, 5% reported one, and only 1% reported two or more.

In Table 85 the number of warning signs experienced by male

Table 85: Number of Warning Signs Experienced, by Quantity-Frequency Index (in per cent)

	Male Students Who Drink Quantity-Frequency Index			
Number Experienced	1	2–3	4–5	Total
None	32	35	33	100
One	13	34	53	100
Two	5	23	72	100
Three or four	0	22	78	100

students is seen to be closely related to the quantity-frequency index; 78% of the students who had experienced 3 or more warning signs had Q-F indices of 4 or 5, compared with only 33% of those who had experienced none of the signs. A similar relationship of this experience to the social complications scale is shown in Table 86. Of the students who had experienced none of the warning signs 78% had a complications score of zero (no complications) and

Table 86: Number of Warning Signs Experienced, by Social Complications Scale (in per cent)

	Male Students Who Drink Social Complications Scale			
Number Experienced	0	1–2	3–4	Total
None	78	20	2	100
One	55	40	5	100
Two	31	44	25	100
Three or four	18	36	46	100

only 2% had scores of 3 or 4. On the other hand only 18% of the students who had experienced 3 or more of the warning signs had a complications score of zero, and nearly half had scores of 3 or 4.

The warning sign drinkers and the other students were also compared according to responses to a few of the reasons for drinking. As might be expected, 39% of those with 3 or more warning signs, and only 9% of those with no warning signs, indicated that "to get drunk" was an important reason for drinking; 43 and 13% respectively drink "for a sense of well-being." In both instances warning sign drinkers are most inclined to place importance on motivations suggesting psychological dependence or asocial behavior. On the other hand fewer (54%) of those in the group having 3 or more warning signs than of those with no warning signs (65%) listed "to comply with custom" as an important reason.

Anxiety about Drinking

The final questions to be considered in this chapter were concerned not specifically with behavior which might suggest potential problem drinking but rather with indications of anxiety over the effects of drinking and its possible consequences.

Anxiety over drinking was expressed by 17% of the men and 10% of the women student drinkers; these reported that they either feared the long-range consequences of their drinking, or had felt that they might become dependent on or addicted to drink, or both (Table 87). These students, whom we shall designate for con-

Table 87: Students Expressing Anxiety over Consequences of Drinking (in per cent)

	Students Who Drink	
	Men	Women
Have feared long-range consequences of drinking	16	8
Have felt might become dependent on or addicted to use of alcoholic beverages	8	4
Either or both of above	17	10

venience as "anxious drinkers," have been compared with all other users, whom we shall call "secure drinkers," according to a number of criteria.

Anxiety does not necessarily stem from excessive drinking or from unfortunate personal experience. More than 90% of the students, we remember, had received some advice about alcohol, and nearly half reported that this advice was designed to make them abstainers. A review of text materials and the literature on alcohol that are designed for young people reveals that much of the formal advice provided through school or church is based on a psychology of fear. It is to be expected that the degree of concern over drinking will in part reflect the drinking sanctions to which the individual has been subjected. The student who has been brought up to believe that even moderate drinking is wrong or harmful may well experience much greater anxiety over consumption of very slight amounts of alcohol than the student who occasionally drinks to excess but comes from an environment where drinking is part of the accepted and expected social pattern.

It was found that advice to abstain had been received by 54% of the anxious male drinkers and only 43% of the secure drinkers; by 50% of the anxious and only 40% of the secure female users. This suggests that for some students anxiety may in part result from advice they have received against drinking. This could explain the anxiety of those students whose own drinking patterns have given them little real reason for concern. For example, it was found that among the anxious drinkers a fourth of the males and three-fourths of the females had never been drunk; half of these men and two-thirds of these women had never had drinking complications. Although these particular anxious drinkers do not appear to have a basis in personal drinking experience for fearing the consequences of their drinking, anxiety is seen to increase in direct proportion to the extent of the experience of drinking complications. While anxious drinkers represent only 12% of the men who have never been drunk, they constitute 27% of those drunk more than 5 times. Of the men with no social complications only 13% are anxious drinkers, compared with 22% of those with few complications (score of 1 or 2) and 40% of those with more frequent complications (score of 3 or 4). Anxious drinkers included 44% of the students who had experienced at least three of the four warning signs, compared with 20% of those who had experienced one or two of them and only 4% of the students who reported none.

Some anxiety over drinking appears to reflect instruction about alcohol which was couched in terms of threat and fear. However, in the majority of cases where anxiety is expressed by men, it is associated with a relatively high incidence of intoxication, of difficulties resulting from drinking, or of warning signs of potential problem drinking. This is a highly significant finding, for it suggests that the potential problem drinker begins to recognize something different about his own drinking behavior and is often fearful of the consequences at a relatively early stage of development. It has long been recognized that prerequisites to recovery from alcoholism include the acknowledgment that a serious problem exists and sufficient concern over the problem to motivate a desire for change. It has sometimes been claimed that the problem drinker could not be helped until he reached a stage where drastic consequences jolted him into recognition of the seriousness of his condition. The data of our college study suggest that a large segment of those students whose drinking patterns display some of the warning signs are already, when still quite young, worried about the consequences of their drinking. Constructive counseling at this early stage might contribute effectively toward preventing future progression into alcoholism.

Summary

This chapter has examined in student drinking a number of factors which alcoholics have reported retrospectively as characteristic of their incipient problem drinking: the extent to which student drinkers have become involved in various difficulties as a result of drinking, the incidence of special stress on the importance of drinking, and a group of characteristic warning signs of potential problem drinking.

For most of the students who reported any of the complications or warning signs, the experiences were infrequent and often but a single incident; they may have been serious problems at the moment but certainly were not indicative of a pattern. However, a high degree of correlation was found between various warning signs and such factors as the frequency and quantity of drinking, the psychological importance of drinking, and the incidence of complications resulting from drinking.

Because the causes of alcoholism are not known, positive identification of the disorder in its incipient stages is not possible. A careful analysis of characteristic forms of behavior, such as those we have examined here, should make it possible to develop indices for prediction. Properly handled, these might serve as a tool for effective health education, leading not only to early correction but also to that final goal, prevention. From the findings of our study we may venture a guess that 6% of the male student drinkers and at most 1% of the women manifest positive signs of being potential problem drinkers. It is at least suggestive that our analysis reveals the same sex differential that is found in descriptions of the alcoholic population. Perhaps a small fraction of these students who are potential problem drinkers would already be diagnosed as alcoholics. But it must be stressed that positive diagnoses or identification of alcoholism or even of potential alcoholism would require both intensive study of individual cases and careful follow-up over periods of years. It is hoped that the findings of this study can be followed up. Only by that means can this first attempt to identify potential problem drinking be evaluated and more refined measures be developed.

More immediate and positive significance can be attached to the findings on anxiety over drinking. The fact that large proportions of those students with extreme drinking patterns, more frequent complications, and warning signs are concerned with the long-range consequences of their drinking suggests a susceptibility to constructive counseling aimed at preventing progression into serious pathological drinking. Although our results are not conclusive, the combination of the two tentative findings of this chapter— that incipient cases can be detected and are susceptible to treatment—gives perhaps the best grounds for optimism about the problem of alcoholism yet reported by serious research.

CHAPTER 13. *What Students Think*
About Drinking

In our analysis of drinking in college so far we have been concerned primarily with actual behavior, with certain measurable background factors, and with students' perceptions of the pressures, attitudes, and reasons governing their own personal drinking practices. We shall turn now to another body of information significant for the over-all evaluation of college drinking patterns: student attitudes toward drinking by others. We asked students the extent to which they thought girls and boys of college age and men and women should drink. We inquired about their reaction to abstainers, both those who make no issue of their abstention and those who try to influence the behavior of others. One question dealt with reactions to drunkenness in other persons of both sexes. Another inquired about "behavior associated with drinking which you think is going too far," again differentiating men and women. Finally, students were asked to indicate their reaction toward "the double standard which generally allows greater license in drinking behavior to men than to women."

We have already alluded to the confusion that often characterizes opinions and explanations about human customs. This is particularly marked in areas which have undergone any considerable degree of change. Attitudes usually change more slowly than the overt or material aspects of behavior; as a result, notions developed earlier to explain behavior of a previous period may be retained to explain new ways with which they are really not compatible. As we have noted, despite a marked change in types of alcoholic beverages consumed in the United States during the last century, many contemporary explanations of drinking behavior are offered in terms of the 19th century's consumption patterns. The Americans of Italian origin who associate with their present beer drinking the symbolic meaning and interpretations which were developed to explain the custom of drinking wine are an example. And so, in the present chapter, we shall consider the degree to which student attitudes toward drinking seem consistent with their own drinking behavior, and whether these attitudes, like their behavior, are associated with such factors as religion and family income. Finally, we shall compare actual practice and opinion with respect to a particular aspect of drinking, the double standard which prescribes different degrees of drinking license for men and for women.

Extent to Which Others Should Drink

In questions on the extent to which others should drink, students were asked to check a list offering several alternative categories ranging from "not at all" to "anything and as much as they please." Table 88 shows that both male and female students grant license in drinking in decreasing order to men, boys of college age, women, and girls of college age.

For all students, most variation occurs in the extreme attitudes. Roughly three-fifths of the students would permit drinking in moderation for each of the four categories. Both males and females would allow greater freedom to women than to girls of college age, and to men than to boys of college age. Both also display a marked double standard for the sexes, permitting more freedom in drinking to boys of college age than to their female contemporaries and greater freedom to men than to women. We shall return to this question later on.

In considering possible relationships between attitudes toward drinking and other factors, we shall limit ourselves to students who feel that girls of college age should not drink at all. Table 89 shows the percentage of students, according to religious affiliation, who believe girls should abstain. Seventy per cent of the Mormon male students feel girls should not drink, compared with but a third of the Protestants, and very few of the Catholics or Jews. An even greater contrast appears in the opinions of the girls, ranging from

83% of the Mormons down to only 2% of the Jews. These expressions of attitude by students of different religious faiths are strikingly consistent with the extent to which they accept or reject drinking as a custom. This is especially true in the case of the Mormon and Jewish groups, which have clear-cut sanctions in this regard. The girls are also consistent in attitude and behavior. In fact more Catholic, Jewish, and Protestant girls abstain them-

Table 88: Attitudes toward Drinking (in per cent)

| | Opinion of Male Students Extent to Which the Following Should Drink | | | |
	Girls of College Age	Women	Boys of College Age	Men
Not at all	34	24	20	16
Beer or wine only	7	6	11	6
Moderation	54	62	58	62
Anything and as much as they please	5	8	11	16
Total	100	100	100	100

| | Opinion of Female Students Extent to Which the Following Should Drink | | | |
	Girls of College Age	Women	Boys of College Age	Men
Not at all	33	27	25	22
Beer or wine only	6	6	8	7
Moderation	58	63	61	63
Anything and as much as they please	3	4	6	8
Total	100	100	100	100

Table 89: Attitude toward Drinking, by Religious Affiliation (in per cent)

| Religious Affiliation | Students in Each Religious Group Who Indicate That Girls of College Age Should Abstain | |
	Male	Female
Jewish	9	2
Catholic	16	13
Protestant	36	32
Mormon	70	83

selves than feel that other girls of college age should abstain
(Table 90).

Table 90: Drinking Practice and Attitude of College Girls, by Religious Affiliation (in per cent)

Religious Affiliation	Girls Who Abstain	Girls Indicating That Girls of College Age Should Abstain
Jewish	6	2
Catholic	22	13
Protestant	40	32
Mormon	77	83

We have seen that the incidence of drinking is related to economic status, and that students with higher family incomes are
a good deal more apt to be users of alcoholic beverages than those
in the low income brackets. A similar relationship exists between
income and attitude toward drinking by girls. Table 91 shows

Table 91: Attitude toward Drinking, by Family Income (in per cent)

| Family Income | Students in Each Income Group Indicating That Girls of College Age Should Abstain | |
	Male	Female
Under $2,500	49	63
$2,500–$4,999	35	44
$5,000–$9,999	27	34
$10,000 and over	14	12

that the percentage of male students who feel that girls should
abstain ranges from only 14% of those with family incomes of
$10,000 or more to half of those with incomes under $2,500. Attitudes of female students show a similar relationship to income.
We also find that within each income category there are more
girls who abstain than who feel that other girls of college age in
general should abstain (Table 92).

In a comparison of attitudes according to type of college sharp contrasts again appear (Table 93). Students at private nonsectarian colleges for men or women only are the most liberal, followed by those at private, nonsectarian, coeducational schools and those at public colleges with a general curriculum. It should also be noted that at the types of college where liberal attitudes prevail more girls would allow liberality than boys. On the other

Table 92: *Comparison for College Girls of Actual Abstaining and Attitude toward Abstaining by Girls, by Family Income (in per cent)*

Family Income	College Girls Who Abstain	College Girls Indicating That Girls of College Age Should Abstain
Under $2,500	70	63
$2,500–$4,999	52	44
$5,000–$9,999	42	34
$10,000 and over	21	12

hand, at private "dry" colleges, public teachers' colleges, and southern Negro colleges, where prohibitions are strongest, girls are as apt to impose restrictions as boys, or more so.

Opinions on the extent to which girls should drink were also compared with drinking behavior (Table 94). While only 33% of the female students in the study feel that girls of college age should not drink, 39% are themselves abstainers. Of those who abstain three-fourths feel that girls in general should abstain,

Table 93: *Attitude toward Drinking, by Type of College (in per cent)*

Type of College	Students Indicating That Girls of College Age Should Abstain	
	Male	Female
Pvt., men or women only, nonsect.	5	2
Pvt., coed., nonsect.	14	7
Pvt., coed., "dry"	57	56
Pub., coed., general	30	18
Pub., coed., teachers	51	60
Pub., coed., southern Negro	46	53

an opinion held by only 6% of the girls who drink. Seventy-nine
per cent of the college boys who abstain feel that girls of college
age should not drink, compared with 17% of the boys who drink.
Among male students who drink, responses to the opinion question varied according to quantity-frequency ratings. Students who
believe girls should not drink ranged from 39% of those with
a low Q-F rating of 1 down to only 4% of those with a high Q-F
rating of 5.

*Table 94: Attitude toward Drinking, by Ab-
stinence or Use and Quantity-Frequency
(in per cent)*

Students Who Feel That Girls
of College Age Should Abstain

MALE

Abstainers	79
All Users	17
According to Q-F index	
Q-F 1	39
2	26
3	16
4	15
5	4

FEMALE

Abstainers	73
All Users	6
According to Q-F index	
Q-F 1	8
2	0

Thus far we have seen that the distribution of college students
who feel that girls of college age should not drink varies according to religious affiliation, family income, and type of college. We
have also seen that actual drinking by most college boys and girls
is consistent with their attitudes toward drinking by girls. So we
have not found a marked pattern of inconsistency between behavior and attitude. On the contrary, the evidence suggests quite
close agreement at this particular level.

Reaction to Abstainers

We turn now to the students' reactions toward those abstainers who make no point of their abstention and those who try to influence the behavior of others. A check list of possible reactions was provided. The distribution of responses according to sex appears in Table 95.

Table 95: Attitude toward Abstainers (in per cent)

Attitude of Students toward Abstainers Who	Make No Point of Their Abstention		Try to Influence the Behavior of Others	
			Attitudes of	
	Men	Women	Men	Women
Indifference	40	32	28	27
Admiration, approval, respect	54	62	24	25
Derogation, disapproval, resentment, scorn	4	4	46	46
Pity	2	2	2	2
Total	100	100	100	100

Well over half the students expressed admiration, respect, or approval for the abstainer who minds his own business, 40% of the males and 32% of the females were indifferent, and only 4% resented or rejected him. On the other hand, only one in four approved the abstainer who tries to influence others, while nearly half rejected him. Furthermore, a substantial segment of students who are indifferent to or even admire or respect the abstainer who makes no point of his abstention expressed disapproval, resentment, or scorn for the abstainer who tries to influence others. Actually, more than 40% of the students of each sex accept the quiet abstainer but express rejection of the militant "dry."

Reaction toward the militant abstainer is related to religious affiliation (Table 96). Roughly half the Mormon students admire, approve, or respect him, as compared with only about 10% of the Jews and a fourth of the Protestants. The lowest income groups are most apt to approve, while the highest will more frequently resent or disapprove (Table 97).

Attitudes toward the abstainer who tries to reform others also

Table 96: *Attitude toward Abstainer Who Tries to Influ-*
ence the Behavior of Others, by Religious Affiliation
(in per cent)

Religious Affiliation	Admiration, Approval, Respect		Derogation, Disapproval, Resentment, Scorn	
	Male	Female	Male	Female
Jewish	10	9	57	41
Catholic	17	7	49	44
Protestant	29	23	43	43
Mormon	49	54	29	27

Table 97: *Attitude toward Abstainer Who Tries to Influ-*
ence the Behavior of Others, by Family Income (in
per cent)

Family Income	Admiration, Approval, Respect		Derogation, Disapproval, Resentment, Scorn	
	Male	Female	Male	Female
Under $2,500	36	43	36	31
$2,500–$4,999	26	36	46	29
$5,000–$9,999	26	19	43	45
$10,000 and over	17	9	58	52

vary markedly according to personal drinking practices (Table
98). Admiration, respect, or approval was expressed by 57% of the
male abstainers, by only 18% of the users with lower Q-F ratings,

Table 98: *Attitude toward Abstainer Who Tries to In-*
fluence the Behavior of Others, by Abstinence and
Use (in per cent)

Male	Admiration, Approval, Respect	Derogation, Disapproval, Resentment, Scorn
Abstainer	57	24
User Q-F 1–3	18	45
User Q-F 4–5	12	60
Female		
Abstainer	44	26
User Q-F 1	14	47
User Q-F 2	3	62

and by only 12% of the users with high Q-F ratings. At the same time disapproval, resentment, or scorn was expressed by 60% of the men with high Q-F ratings, 45% of those with low Q-F ratings, and 24% of the abstainers. College women resemble college men in the relationship between their actual drinking behavior and their attitude toward the militant abstainer.

Reactions expressed toward abstainers clearly indicate that, when they think about it, students have a rather wholesome respect for the individual who in his own quiet way prefers not to drink; the vast majority, abstainers and drinkers alike, either approve, respect, or are indifferent to his decision. On the other hand, a sizable segment of students, including even a fourth of those who themselves abstain, reject or resent the abstainer who tries to induce others to follow his example. Discussions of this question on many campuses indicate that although students usually do not recognize their own tolerance for the inoffensive abstainer, they clearly recognize the stigma incurred by the "dry" abstainer. They often unthinkingly generalize this stigma to apply to all students who abstain, and assume that the student who doesn't drink is a proponent, whether he says so or not, of total abstinence. On some campuses this stigma and its thoughtless application to all abstainers exert tremendous pressure to drink on students who feel that drinking is a prerequisite for general social acceptance. Thus, ironically enough, the militant dry has had a share in forcing potential abstainers to participate in the drinking custom. At many colleges the stigma attached to his "holier than thou" attitude has made others eager to avoid his label. In this area lies one of the real challenges to planners of education about alcohol. Those who wish to abstain need the courage of their convictions and the support which may come through a greater understanding by everyone of the nature of drinking customs and of the pressures and sanctions which surround them. It is encouraging to find that few students intellectually reject the inoffensive abstainer; but unfortunately this is an area where emotion often rules over reason. Through constructive education we may hope to reverse this emotional imbalance and to reduce the attendant confusion.

Reaction to Drunkenness

Students were asked to indicate their reaction to drunkenness in others, both of the same and the opposite sex. A check list of ten responses was provided (Table 99). Male and female students

Table 99: *Reaction of Students toward Drunkenness in Others (in per cent)*

Male Attitudes toward Drunkenness in	Men	Women
Indifference	15	5
Tolerance	18	6
Pity, desire to help	19	14
Disgust, intolerance, scorn, loss of respect	40	72
Amusement	8	3
Fear	—*	—*
Total	100	100

Female Attitudes toward Drunkenness in	Men	Women
Indifference	6	3
Tolerance	9	3
Pity, desire to help	15	18
Disgust, intolerance, scorn, loss of respect	64	74
Amusement	3	2
Fear	3	—*
Total	100	100

* $<0.5\%$.

are in general agreement in their reactions to drunkenness in women. Nearly three-fourths feel disgust, intolerance, scorn, or loss of respect; others feel pity or a desire to help, while very few are tolerant. Female students are almost as intolerant of drunkenness in men. Male students, however, appear more willing to accept drunkenness in their own sex. Only 40% of the males indicate rejection of drunkenness in men, compared with 72% who frowned on drunkenness in women; 33% are tolerant or indifferent to drunkenness in their own sex, compared with only 11% tolerant or indifferent to drunkenness in women.

Male reactions to drunkenness in men show some relationship to income and religion. Men with family incomes under $2,500 are less apt than those from families having incomes of $10,000 or more to be indifferent or tolerant toward drunkenness, and somewhat more apt to express reactions of disapproval or rejection. No marked differences in attitude toward drunkenness in men appear among Catholic, Jewish, and Protestant men. Mormons, however, as compared with the other three, are significantly less tolerant (Table 100).

Table 100: Reaction of Male Students toward Drunkenness in Other Men, by Religious Affiliation (in per cent)

	Tolerance or Indifference	Disgust, Intolerance, Scorn, Loss of Respect
Mormon	21	47
Jewish	34	37
Catholic	36	34
Protestant	36	39

Male students who are abstainers are less tolerant than users; and among users those with high Q-F ratings display the greatest degree of tolerance toward drunkenness (Table 101). Students who

Table 101: Reaction of Male Students toward Drunkenness in Other Men, by Abstinence or Extent of Use (in per cent)

	Tolerance or Indifference	Disgust, Intolerance, Scorn, Loss of Respect
Abstainer	15	48
User, Q-F 1–3	37	44
User, Q-F 4–5	46	26

themselves have been drunk are much less apt to react against drunkenness in others than those who have never been drunk. Still, a fourth of those who have themselves experienced more than an isolated incident of drunkenness disapprove of drunkenness in others (Table 102).

The Double Standard

It is obvious that all students, but particularly males, are much more tolerant of drunkenness in men than in women. Actually 38% of the males and 10% of the females displayed this form of

Table 102: Reaction of Male Users toward Drunkenness in Other Men, by Times Drunk (in per cent)

Times Drunk	Tolerance or Indifference	Disgust, Intolerance, Scorn, Loss of Respect
Never	33	47
Once	44	41
More than once	47	25

double standard. Other expressions of double standard were found in the questions on the extent to which others should drink. A fourth of the men and 15% of the women allowed boys greater freedom in drinking than girls; and similar numbers allowed men greater freedom than women.

An additional measure of the double standard was found in the request to specify, for both sexes, behavior associated with drinking which one thinks is "going too far." Responses to this question were rated by the survey staff for specific indications of double standard, and it was found that fully two-thirds of the men and half the women allowed greater latitude of behavior to men before adjudging it "going too far." For example, a student who thinks that men are going too far when they manifest "inability to walk or nausea" feels that "loud or coarse behavior" is unacceptable in women. Another who specifies "getting drunk" for men lists merely "getting silly" for women. Still another who lists "loss of control of self" for men says that "drinking itself is going too far" for women. About a third of the students mentioned some form of sexual behavior as "going too far." This will be discussed in the next chapter.

In addition to four questions in which responses could be measured for an indication that the double standard is practiced, students were asked specifically about their personal reaction to the double standard itself—to society's generally allowing greater license in drinking behavior to men than to women. Five possible responses were provided. In Table 103 a comparison of responses according to sex shows, as would be expected, that male students are much more apt than women to approve the double

Table 103: Reaction to Double Standard Which Prescribes Greater License in Drinking to Men Than to Women (in per cent)

	Men	Women
Indifference	31	39
Resentment, disapproval	19	27
Approval	45	31
Amusement	5	3
Total	100	100

standard which accords them greater license. Yet it is significant that three out of ten women also approve it and that more women approve than resent or disapprove.

Data on the double standard provide an opportunity to measure the consistency between actual overt behavior and common explanations for that behavior. Answers to questions on the extent to which others should drink, on reactions to drunkenness, and on behavior which is going too far all indicate acceptance or rejection of the double standard in practice. The question about personal reaction to the concept of the double standard provides a measure of the explanation or justification or of what the students think their double standard practice is. On the basis of actual practice, students can be grouped into five categories, ranging from those whose answers displayed a positive double standard on each of four possible occasions down to those who displayed none. Students in each of these groups can then be considered in terms of their explanation or rationalization (Table 104). Some confusion is indicated by the fact that 6% of the students who at every opportunity demonstrated that they practice the double standard, along with 8% of those who practiced it on three of four occasions, believe that they disapprove or resent it. At the same time, 21% of those who never displayed the double standard and

42% who displayed it only once nevertheless expressed approval.

However, the consistency and agreement shown between overt expression and personal interpretation are much more impressive. Comparatively few of the students who practiced the double standard think that they disapprove, while more than half of those who practice it recognize that they approve it.

Table 104: Practice of Double Standard, by Reaction toward It (in per cent)

Students Demonstrating Practice of Double Standard in Their Responses to	Expression of Personal Reaction to Double Standard	
	Approval	Disapproval, Resentment
Four items	69	6
Three items	63	8
Two items	50	15
One item	42	18
None	21	44

Summary

In the various measures of opinion and attitude which we have examined there appears to be a fairly high degree of consistency between the student's own drinking behavior and his interpretation of the degree of drinking which he would prescribe for others. The abstainer is most likely and the heavy drinker least likely to feel that others should not drink, to approve the militant abstainer, and to condemn drunkenness in others. The attitudes of groups of different religion and income level also tend to vary in conformity to differences already observed in their drinking practices. The findings do not reveal the expected degree of confusion between overt practice and attitude which has been described as common to drinking behavior in American society. There is more consistency than confusion between the actual demonstration and the interpretation of behavior relating to the double standard.

Yet several specific areas of confusion and emotion are revealed. Men are equally divided between sympathy and rejection in their reaction toward drunkenness in other men. Equal numbers of women report approval and resentment of the double standard. Nearly all students are able to express an intellectual acceptance of the abstainer who minds his own business, but many reject the nondrinker who would impose his own beliefs on others, and the emotional impact of this rejection is frequently generalized in practice to apply to all abstainers. It is possible that students, either because of a higher than average intelligence level or because as a generation they escaped the full force of the conflict about national Prohibition, are better able than some to evaluate behavior and attitudes in this area realistically. Furthermore, they have not yet been subjected to the highly emotional impact of adult responsibilities. They are not for the most part parents or church leaders. They do not occupy positions of responsibility in the community. In short, they do not fill certain types of role which would be apt to conflict morally with their personal drinking practices. And it should be remembered that while there is a surprising consistency of drinking behavior and attitudes of college students on the intellectual level, this consistency does not always extend to those aspects of the custom which are most highly charged with emotion.

CHAPTER 14. *Beliefs about Drinking*
and Sexual Behavior

Speaking of drinking and sexual behavior, the porter in Shakespeare's *Macbeth* remarks: "Lechery, sir, it provokes, and unprovokes; it provokes the desire, but it takes away the performance; therefore, much drink may be said to be an equivocator with lechery."

Alcohol, as we have seen, is a depressant which has the psychological effect of relaxing inhibitions. Of all the inhibitions imposed on individuals by our society, those in the sphere of sexual activity are among the strongest. And those members of the society who are attending college are among the most stringently restricted in these forms of behavior.[1] To the extent that it lowers anxieties and tensions sometimes associated with sexual behavior, alcohol may facilitate the temporary lowering of barriers to sexual activity. It should not be assumed that it will necessarily or always have this effect. Far from it. The act of drinking alcoholic beverages, it is clear from the student responses described in this chapter, can itself specifically provoke anxiety about sexual behavior. The very act of drinking or the intent to drink may immediately activate increased anxieties and controls; this effect will vary with individuals and with situations. It does not, of course, alter the depressant function of alcohol, but it does alter the immediate psychological state upon which the depressant is to operate, and hence is an effective modifier of behavior. The relaxing and

1. A. C. Kinsey, W. B. Pomeroy, and C. E. Martin, *Sexual Behavior in the Human Male* (Philadelphia, W. B. Saunders Co. 1948), pp. 374–386.

tension-lowering functions of alcohol are effective with small amounts, and their effect increases to a point of eventual unconsciousness if the amount of alcohol in the body continues to increase. Large amounts of alcohol, as the porter pointed out, at least in males have the physiological result of temporary impotence.[2]

We have just seen that substantial numbers of students, both male and female, would allow a greater degree of freedom in drinking to men or boys than to women or girls. One of the basic beliefs underlying this double standard is illustrated by statements on the types of behavior students associate with drinking which "goes too far." About a third of these comments concerned morally unacceptable sexual behavior, either implying or explicitly stating the belief that drinking by women is associated with increased vulnerability to sexual advances.

Of the male students who described "going too far" in terms of sexual behavior, about eight out of ten did so only for women; they described going too far for men in terms of violence. For example, the following are typical statements by ten men about behavior they consider going too far in connection with drinking:

Among Men	*Among Women*
1. Reckless driving and abusing others	1. Sexual misbehavior
2. Swearing and profane language	2. Acting loose in morals
3. Offensiveness	3. Sex promiscuity
4. Becoming violent	4. Not knowing what they are doing in affairs with men
5. Fighting	5. Flirting
6. Fighting	6. Petting
7. Sexual intercourse	7. Sexual intercourse
8. When they get out of hand	8. When they get sexy
9. Robbing, stealing, gang fights	9. Sexual intercourse
10. Intercourse	10. Intercourse

On the other hand, most of the women who specified sexual activity as "going too far" did so for both sexes. Here are typical statements from ten women:

2. See C. S. Ford and F. A. Beach, *Patterns of Sexual Behavior* (New York, Harper, 1952), pp. 237–238.

Among Men	*Among Women*
1. Loose in morals	1. Loose in morals
2. Fighting, public necking	2. Necking all over
3. Petting and sexual intercourse	3. Petting and sexual intercourse
4. Lovemaking	4. Making passes at men
5. Too familiar and coarse	5. Sexual promiscuity
6. Taking advantage of situations with female companions	6. Arouses sexual behavior
7. Trying to force one to neck with you	7. Necking too much
8. Hanging on girls	8. Petting and intercourse
9. Necking and passionate kissing	9. Vulgar acting
10. Petting and sexual intercourse	10. Having anything to do with men

Discussions with students brought out further that many boys and girls hold the common belief that girls who drink may appear to be more popular with men but often are not taken seriously or respected: one can have a good time with a girl who drinks but may not consider her as a future wife. The belief is substantiated by the findings on the drinking and dating habits of 336 women in a coeducational college. "Regular" drinkers (at least 3 times within the preceding 2 weeks) had far exceeded less frequent drinkers or abstainers in frequency of dates with men but were not nearly as apt to be "engaged, pinned or going steady with a young man." [3]

Actually we are dealing here not only with a double standard for drinking but also with one for sexual activity, which generally allows greater freedom of action to men than to women in socially questionable sexual behavior. Also, we should continue to bear in mind that most women usually drink in mixed company while a large proportion of college men do much of their drinking, especially the heavier drinking, in all-male gatherings. Most of the women, therefore, to the extent that their attitudes are related to experience, are appraising drinking and undesirable behavior for situations in which both sexes are present. Men, on the other hand, think of "going too far" in two contexts: in mixed groups,

3. Carol A. Hecht, Ruth J. Grine, and Sally E. Rothrock. "The Drinking and Dating Habits of 336 College Women in a Coeducational Institution," *Quarterly Journal of Studies on Alcohol 9* (September 1948), 252–258.

when they consider women; usually in male gatherings when they consider men's—especially heavier—drinking.

Not included in our survey but obviously relevant to this discussion is the matter of what constitutes going too far in sexual activity. Some students may feel that for unmarried college students any sexual activity is going too far. If the same individuals also feel that drinking itself is going too far, a correlation of the two beliefs is to be expected.

Independent of the question about going too far in either sexual or drinking behavior, three direct questions on beliefs about drinking and sexual behavior were included in the survey. Students were asked whether they believe that drinking generally 1) accompanies or facilitates petting and necking, 2) precipitates feelings of sexual excitement, and 3) accompanies or facilitates sexual intercourse. The distributions of alternative responses (yes, no, or no opinion) are shown in Table 105. Nearly a third of the women and half the men believe that drinking is generally associated with sexual intercourse; half of all the students believe

Table 105: Distribution of Beliefs on Relationship between Drinking and Sexual Behavior (in per cent)

	All Students	
Do you feel that drinking generally:	Men	Women
Accompanies or facilitates petting and necking?		
Yes	63	54
No	16	15
No opinion	21	31
Total	100	100
Precipitates feelings of sexual excitement?		
Yes	51	51
No	25	15
No opinion	24	34
Total	100	100
Accompanies or facilitates sexual intercourse?		
Yes	47	31
No	23	20
No opinion	30	49
Total	100	100

that it usually precipitates feelings of sexual excitement, and more than half assume that it usually accompanies or facilitates petting and necking. Relatively few students (under 25% in all cases) believe that drinking is *not* generally associated with these various levels of sexual behavior. The girls are somewhat less likely than the boys to associate drinking with sexual activity and more apt to express no opinion on these questions.

When all three questions are considered together, 69% of the men and 62% of the women believe that drinking is associated with at least one level of sex behavior, and 36% of the men and 27% of the women replied yes to all three questions. These findings are further indication of a widespread belief that alcohol has an important function in sex play and sexual intercourse. The effect of this belief on anxieties and self-controls has already been mentioned. Whether there is an actual relationship between the two and, if so, whether this is a causal relationship are matters not covered by the survey. The belief itself, however, would seem to be a significant factor modifying behavior.

A distinct relationship was found between the probability that a student would associate drinking with sexual behavior and his or her own drinking pattern. Table 106 shows for abstainers, and for users classified by the Q-F index, the percentages of stu-

Table 106: Association of Drinking with Sexual Behavior, by Extent of Drinking (in per cent)

| | Students Who Associate Drinking with | | | |
	Petting and Necking	Sexual Excitement	Sexual Intercourse	At Least One Form of Sex Behavior
Men				
Abstainers	61	48	54	69
Users Q-F 1	55	42	41	61
2	63	41	41	68
3	58	52	43	65
4	67	54	49	73
5	87	73	58	92
Women				
Abstainers	53	47	33	61
Users Q-F 1	55	56	25	64
2	81	75	35	85

dents who replied yes to each of the questions relating to drinking and sexual behavior and of those replying yes to at least one question. By each measure students with high Q-F ratings are found most likely to associate drinking with sexual activity. Yet at least three out of five students, users and abstainers, men and women, see some relationship between drinking and sexual behavior, and abstainers reply yes on the intercourse question almost as frequently as the highest Q-F users.

These distributions of response suggest that beliefs about drinking and sex may involve two quite independent factors: experience and moral indoctrination. Abstainers who associate drinking with sexual behavior obviously are not basing their belief on drinking experience. We have seen that Mormon and Protestant abstainers report more frequent religious participation than do users, and that regardless of affiliation young people who are most active in religious matters are most responsive to religious sanctions against drinking. Kinsey, Pomeroy, and Martin report that young people who are most active in religious functions are least active sexually.[4] We suggest therefore that abstainers who associate drinking with sexual activity reflect consciously or otherwise a form of moral indoctrination which may be closely related to their abstinence from both drinking and sexual activity. When students' responses to questions on drinking and sexual activity are compared by religious affiliation, no significant differences are found among users, but among abstainers Mormons are most apt to associate drinking and sexual behavior, followed by Protestants and then Catholics. For example, two-thirds of the Mormon abstainers associate drinking with sexual intercourse, compared with 54% of the Protestant abstainers, 42% of the Catholic abstainers, and about 46% of the users in each religious group. Whereas moral indoctrination may also influence the beliefs of students who drink, the rise in incidence of affirmative responses for high Q-F drinkers suggests that these beliefs may reflect actual experience for the heaviest and most frequent drinkers.

We do not have data on students' sexual activity nor are we able to differentiate between those students who feel that drinking is related to unacceptable sexual behavior and those who believe that

4. Pp. 469–473.

drinking also accompanies or facilitates morally acceptable sexual behavior. However, some relevant insights can be gained by comparing the responses of married and single students. Table 107

Table 107: Association of Drinking with Sexual Behavior, by Marital Status (in per cent)

	Students Who Associate Drinking with		
Men	Petting and Necking	Sexual Excitement	Sexual Intercourse
Married	69	54	67
Single	63	51	43
Women			
Married	64	64	45
Single	58	54	30

shows that a greater percentage of married students responded yes to all three questions; but on the sexual intercourse question sizable differences appear. Two-thirds of the married men and only 43% of the single men believe that drinking generally accompanies or facilitates sexual intercourse, as do 45% of the married women and only 30% of the single women. When the drinking habits of married and single students are compared the groups are found to contain similar percentages of abstainers and users, but among the users married students drink less frequently and in smaller amounts. (Among the married male users 27% were Q-F 4 or 5 drinkers, among the single ones 47%; among the women 25% of the married users and 30% of the single were Q-F 2.)

The incidence of affirmative responses for married and single men, according to extent of drinking, appears in Table 108.[5] For all three questions, the incidence of yeses among single students is lowest for the moderate drinkers (Q-F 1–3) and much greater for both abstainers and high Q-F drinkers. Among married students this relationship is almost exactly reversed. These differences among light or moderate drinkers are extraordinary: 92% of the married and only 45% of the single relate drinking to petting and

5. The number of married women in the study, when broken down into use categories, was too small for significant analysis in this connection.

necking; 63% and 37% respectively relate it to feelings of sexual excitement; 88% of the married and only 25% of the single associate it with sexual intercourse. We have not been able to dis-

Table 108: *Association of Drinking with Sexual Behavior, by Quantity-Frequency Index for Male Married and Single Students*

| | Students Who Associate Drinking with | | | | | |
| | Petting and Necking | | Sexual Excitement | | Sexual Intercourse | |
	Married	Single	Married	Single	Married	Single
Abstainers	60	61	51	47	57	53
Users Q-F 1–3	92	45	63	37	88	25
4–5	66	76	66	61	63	49

cover from our data any factor or simple combination of factors (such as age or religion) to explain this difference between the single and the married. The significance appears to rest with the fact of marriage.

This chapter has been concerned so far with beliefs about alcohol and sexual activity. What are the facts about actual behavior in this area? We do not know. The most comprehensive report of what might be termed the biological aspects of sexual behavior in American males does not consider this sociopsychological aspect of sexual behavior.[6] There is no evidence as to the actual relationship between drinking and sexual behavior, although this has in no way hampered the expression of opinions on the subject.

It seems most unlikely that any sweeping generalization, such as that the ingestion of certain amounts of alcohol 1) increases sexual activity or 2) decreases sexual activity or 3) is unrelated to increase or decrease in sexual activity, will ever be formulated by disciplined research on this subject. Such simple, absolute relationships among complex behavioral structures with manifold interrelationships do not exist. Glib explanations of the differential in opinion between the single and married students who are light and occasional drinkers could be presented, assuming either that drinking actually facilitated sexual activity or that it did not. Similarly,

6. Kinsey, Pomeroy, and Martin. They do not report on drinking, although "use of alcohol" is listed as an item covered in the personal histories.

using either assumption, facile interpretations could be made of the fact that, among single students, more of the abstainers and of the frequent and heavier drinkers than of the light, occasional users tended to believe that drinking facilitated sexual intercourse. Such explanations and interpretations, however, must remain intellectual exercises and nothing more, until relevant and verified knowledge is available. But whatever the facts of behavior prove to be, there is no question that beliefs on the subject are widespread, are effective in controlling behavior, and take a variety of often incompatible forms. Recognition of this seems essential for anyone attempting to influence or control drinking behavior.

Summary

In discussing beliefs about sexual activity and drinking, we are dealing simultaneously with two areas of behavior about which great confusion and uncertainty prevail, and individual responses must be interpreted in this light. Some of our data (those pertaining to behavior which is going too far) were obtained indirectly through a question which did not mention sexual activity. The rest were derived from questions which, in retrospect, seem inadequate if for no other reason than that they failed to differentiate between sexual behavior which is morally acceptable and that which is questionable or forbidden according to individual standards. Although our findings suggest many questions which we can only leave for future investigation, certain conclusions can be drawn.

We have found clear evidence of a belief that drinking may be associated with morally questionable sexual behavior and evidence that a double standard exists here. In so far as women are concerned, both sexes are prone to consider "going too far" after drinking in terms of sexual activity alone. For men, "going too far" after drinking is described by women frequently in terms of sexual activity but by men largely in terms of violence. This distinction was in part explained by the different company men and women keep in drinking.

We have found evidence of a widespread belief that drinking generally accompanies various levels of sexual activity. We have no basis for assuming that these beliefs reflect actual behavior—

students were merely asked whether they "feel" that drinking "generally" is associated with sexual activity. However, these prevalent beliefs are in themselves unquestionably significant factors in influencing behavior. Furthermore, the patterns of response according to drinking practice suggest that for some students, particularly the abstainers, such beliefs derive from moral indoctrination of a religious nature and refer to morally unacceptable sexual behavior. How and to what extent experience with necking, petting, and intercourse—both within and without marriage—experience with drinking, and these experiences in combination affected the beliefs about the relation of the two phenomena is not clear. The comparison of single and married light drinkers would indicate that relevant new experience sharply modifies the beliefs stemming from moral indoctrination about the relationship between drinking and sexual behavior. Knowledge of the various beliefs and of the more important factors by which they are modified appears necessary for those who wish to exert rational control over both beliefs and actions related to drinking.

In concluding this chapter it should again be pointed out that the materials relate not to the whole society but only to one age grade in one segment of that society. How important this limitation can be is well illustrated in the matter of sexual behavior. Since the mores restricting sexual intercourse are so much more powerful for the section of society described in this survey [7] than for the rest of the population, the effect of alcohol, whether in increasing anxiety or in allowing release of inhibitions, will probably be different for members of this group than for others. Other things being equal, its capacity to raise anxiety would be greater and its capacity to reduce sexual controls less than for the population at large. It is to be expected that drinking may be significantly related to increased sexual activity in some portions of society but be of little or no importance in increasing such activity in other portions. That it should have a similar effect everywhere in a complex, stratified society is, in the light of existing knowledge of alcohol and human behavior, almost impossible.

7. *Ibid.*, pp. 374–386.

CHAPTER 15. *Drinking as a Custom*

The findings of this study clearly confirm the fact that the drinking of alcoholic beverages is a custom. To understand the effects of using alcohol some knowledge of its chemical structure and physiological and metabolic functions is necessary. But as we have noted, knowledge of the facts about the practice of drinking in a particular society does not automatically follow from this. Drinking customs vary from culture to culture and among the subgroups within one society. The chemistry, physiology, and metabolism of alcohol do not.

In many customs a fairly wide range of variability is available to the individual. Some customs are so loosely structured, poorly integrated with other aspects of the culture, ineffectively transmitted to the next generation, and otherwise lacking in strength that individual variation is fairly extensive. In such cases the individual may determine his own behavior to some extent, although even here he is still heavily influenced by his culture and social surroundings. Even if a Fiji Islander should deviate extremely from a Fijian pattern and a Manhattan Islander from a Manhattan pattern, the cultural origin of the two would still be distinguishable.

The findings of this study emphasize the fact that variations in behavior relating to drinking are closely correlated with such basic social factors as the family, personal associations, religious affiliation, ethnic background, and economic status. We have seen that the individual's behavior with respect to drinking in large measure reflects the behavior patterns of his own social group; and the drinking patterns of college students largely reflect the ways of American society.

We have also seen that the degree of individual deviation from group norms varies inversely with the internal consistency of a given behavior pattern and its integration within the group culture. The Jewish and Mormon drinking customs are extremely different, but each of these groups has a strong, consistent pattern, well integrated with its other customs. Variant drinking behavior, such as drunkenness or its complications, is rare among them. But with other American groups whose drinking customs and attitudes are loosely structured, conflicting, or less definitely transmitted from one generation to the next, variant behavior is much more common.

In one way drinking is a unique behavior. Alcohol temporarily has a direct and measurable effect upon the central nervous system, influencing for a time the individual's total activity. The great majority of its users do not drink enough for their behavior to show much effect. However, large amounts of alcohol consumed in a short period have a marked effect quite different from that which follows excess in other common forms of behavior. Overeating, for example, does not result in a general release of inhibitions or a decrease of muscular controls or sensory perception. Because heavy drinking does, it may lead persons of quite different cultural backgrounds to act very similarly. With the return of sobriety their behavior reverts to normal. However, repeated drinking to the point of intoxication, as in the case of the alcoholic, leads to a withdrawal of the individual from the world around him and to a concurrent withdrawal of society from him, and lessens the influence of the culture on his behavior.

Our survey brought out clearly the relative significance, in molding behavior, of cultural forces as opposed to individual determination. The closest correlations of individual behavior with the cultural norms of social groups were seen in the matter of drinking or not drinking, and in the attitude toward drinking. Factors of family behavior and attitude, religious and ethnic tradition, and economic status all showed a marked and consistent relationship to student behavior and attitude.

Among the drinkers, correlations with sociocultural phenomena were sometimes high, as in the male-female patterns; sometimes not so high, as in the case of choice of beverage and frequency of drinking. The cultural impact was still clear, but often less decisive than in the case of drinking or abstaining.

Among that small proportion who may be called potential problem drinkers most of the correlations with sociocultural factors fell sharply, and individuality was most pronounced.

Perception of drinking as a custom, rather than a biological phenomenon, a matter of individual choice, or an activity determined by some immediate situation, will facilitate understanding the problems which attend it and planning realistically to meet them. Experience has demonstrated that holding high moral values up to the problem drinker will probably not have the desired effect of persuading him to reform; nor will urging the ethical values of a system which proscribes drinking upon a person who is well integrated in another group which does not proscribe drinking. Individual advice to drink or not to drink will have little effect compared to larger sociocultural forces, unless the latter are extremely weak or confused or the individual is but weakly integrated with his group.

Failure to achieve a desired effect does not imply getting no effect; witness the strong negative reactions when student abstainers attempted to alter the behavior of others. But we do not suggest that counseling or urging moral values is useless or invariably works in ways other than those intended. With individuals belonging to a group which prescribes abstinence, setting forth of the group's moral values—their application to everyday life, their relevance to abstinence and incompatibility with drinking—together with a statement of the practical, manifest, and immediate dangers of drinking, will strengthen belief and personal abstinence. Perhaps, even more important, it may also strengthen the influence of the relevant cultural-social forces on the children of the group.

Recognizing drinking as a custom permits another discrimination which can be of great utility in understanding its problems and exerting effective control. Like other customs drinking occurs in many forms, meets a variety of individual and group needs, is accompanied by a variety of attitudes, and is sometimes closely linked with various other aspects of behavior. There is no one form of behavior which is "drinking"; rather there are many forms of drinking custom. So it follows that what may be characteristic of

one form need not be characteristic of the others; and the more
sweeping the generalization about drinking the more likely it is
to be fallacious. Statements that drinking is brutish, is civilized, is
evil, is dangerous, is ritualistic, is convivial, and so on are meaning-
less and perhaps misleading unless both values and specific behavior are understood alike by all parties. For one thing, the values
of speaker and listener may differ; for another, the behavior suggested by the word drinking may have one meaning for the speaker
and another for the listener.

One example of the confusion that attends talking about drinking was the students' frequent question whether using wine or beer
was really "drinking." Participants in the study of Italian-American
drinking practices often reported that they did not drink despite
their unconcealed, daily, and sometimes rather large consumption
of wine or beer. When Americans of Italian extraction hear the
word drink, they are apt to assume that only whisky, rum, or gin
is being discussed.

We have seen wide variation in drinking customs throughout
our survey, in purpose, setting, type of beverage, amounts consumed, and so on. Yet such differences have not been recognized in
the descriptions of drinking as an absolute pattern. If the great
majority of the college students we have reported on are at all
similar to other college students or to other persons, young or old,
it is clear that descriptions of drinking in such absolute fashion are
inaccurate and confusing.

It is not only important to recognize that there is a great variety
of drinking customs; we must also be able to discriminate between
behavior which adheres to a customary pattern and that which,
although similar in some ways, is irrelevant or even antagonistic to
the custom. In describing the custom of "making a living" in our
society, counterfeiting would not ordinarily be used as a typical
example; that is clearly recognized as a deviant form of behavior.
But common conceptions of drinking behavior are frequently illustrated by examples of unusual or deviant aspects of the custom.

The preceding chapters have indicated not only the great variety
of drinking practices in the college community but also the incidence of inadequate, inadvertent, and antisocial behavior: sometimes a single occurrence of a rather mild deviation, sometimes

repeated instances of major deviation. Those among our survey subjects who were drinkers, and many who were not, clearly recognized the difference between acceptable and markedly deviant behavior connected with drinking. But the great majority of formal teachers or rule-setters in education, government, and religion do not appear to make this distinction. Not only has drinking traditionally been defined as an absolute pattern, it has been defined in terms of deviations from the pattern.

To portray drinking as regularly leading to drunkenness, alcoholism, sexual license, accidents and manslaughter, poverty, disgrace, crime, disease, or national calamity is clearly false; no one believes that the 65 to 75 million American drinkers or any large proportion of them meet such fates, to say nothing of its all happening because of drinking. It is exceedingly dangerous to draw such a picture and especially to hold it up to young people. There can be no doubt that many of these problems can be aggravated, and in some instances largely caused, by certain types of drinking. But to describe drinking behavior, to individuals who already are or will shortly become drinkers, only in terms of the most frightening, relatively rare extremes may lead the student to ridicule or deny even the very real dangers.

Of all the students who participated in the survey, only 17% of the men and 6% of the women reported drinking more than once a week. Although frequency alone is hardly an adequate measure of deviation, infrequency of drinking is a pretty fair indication of the absence of marked deviation. Over half the men and more than 70% of the women drank less than once a month or never. That any significant proportion of the users among these students —granted they viewed their own behavior as "drinking"—could accept the supposed facts or philosophies supplied in the lectures, sermons, texts, rulings, or interviews concerning drinking which are generally put before them is beyond credibility. The communications may have had an effect, but probably not the intended one.

This opinion is not meant to reflect on the sincerity of intention of those who present such materials, whether within educational institutions or elsewhere. The trouble lies not with the individuals but in the definition of the task which is given them, in the tools with which they are equipped, and in the value put upon their efforts.

Although the task they are given actually deals with customary behavior, it has been defined in terms of biology, immorality, and rational individual choice. The tools are statements which, upon inquiry, turn out to be largely inaccurate, or to concern noncustomary behavior, or to uphold values which are not those of the audience to whom they are directed. The efforts are valued only by the radical reform movement, which fashioned the tools and which takes its norms from the behavior of only about 25% of those addressed—those who do not drink and who were probably not going to drink anyway. Although this approach may have strengthened the position of the minority of nondrinkers, it does not take into consideration the effect on students who find parts of the message so inconsistent with everyday life and sometimes so ridiculous that they are apt to reject even the very real fact of potential danger in drinking.

Thus, not only is society making an unsatisfactory and unrealistic approach to the problems of alcohol, but the common controls and teachings meet with resistance and sometimes appear to stimulate the very behavior which they are intended to suppress. Some explanation for this can be found in the description of changing patterns of consumption and social responses to alcohol problems given in Chapter 2: in the fact that today's responses are still based on definitions and tools developed during the first half of the 19th century. Explanations of the phenomena of drinking, whether in a political, an economic, or a recreational context, were made then as ethical assertions, usually absolutes, concerning matters of rational individual choice. In the next 50 years biological explanations became increasingly popular and were rapidly added to the intellectual armament of those attempting to explain and control drinking behavior. And meanwhile, in the course of a century, the practice of drinking underwent the striking changes that have been described.

When it is recalled that between 1800 and 1850 the per capita consumption of absolute alcohol was slightly higher than today but a much smaller proportion of the population drank—meaning that those who drank did so heavily and frequently—that drinking was almost entirely in the form of distilled spirits, and that the frontier type of drinking was at its peak, it is not difficult to understand why the Temperance Movement came to consider alcohol, drinking, drunkenness, and alcoholism as one concept, and all productive only of evil. The proportion of instances of drinking accompanied by socially unacceptable behavior was far, far greater then than it is today or has been for generations. But the conception of drinking based on the unfortunate manifestations of 1800 to 1850 remained frozen, so to speak, in the Temperance Movement—and the Temperance Movement was the only movement. No other conceptions based on objective study of custom and behavior and other types of facts have been available for those who have had to deal with the problems of drinking. The power of the movement has been so great that many who are not sympathetic with it, including numbers even in the alcoholic beverage industry, unconsciously accept its definitions of problems.

The importance of the conception of drinking as a custom for those who wish to control or change drinking practices can hardly be overestimated. By means of it, it is possible not only to point out the sterile aspects of an archaic philosophy and its grosser errors but to indicate the direction further inquiry may take and the possibilities for more effective action. With the knowledge that there are levels of drinking behavior dominated by sociocultural forces, other levels which can be manipulated by guidance and the tools of reason, and still other levels that may be reached only by emotional and social restructuring of the individual, it is possible, in the first place, to avoid the waste involved in making every approach on all levels or on the wrong level, which is typical of present activities; and second, to develop techniques for a defined purpose. Ministers, teachers, lawmakers, and others have been continually frustrated in trying to develop better techniques for meeting drinking problems very largely because all three levels have been approached as one. Unfortunately, the more effective a technique is for one level the less effective it is likely to be for the others. Methods useful for controlling the extent of drinking are apt to appear to nondrinkers as invitations to drink. Methods apparently appropriate for alcoholism or for chronic drunkenness are irrelevant for nondrinkers and often rebound with unfortunate effects upon normal drinkers.

That biological forces, individual determination, and ethics are all relevant to drinking is unquestionable; furthermore, all three are relevant to nondrinking and to deviant drinking behavior. However, no one of them can explain drinking, nor can a combination of the three. Seeing drinking as a custom affords a more realistic and broader view, more effective discrimination and insight, and the possibility of developing safer and surer techniques of control.

CHAPTER 16. *The Colleges and Drinking*

When we were considering the title for this book the choice rapidly narrowed to two: College Drinking and Drinking in College. It was suggested that the former was preferable because it was shorter, and because in any event this may very well be referred to as "that book about college drinking." But College Drinking was rejected because there is no evidence that such a phenomenon exists.

Such phrases as night club drinking, frontier drinking, and ritual drinking suggest specific situations, types of participants, purposes, and behavior, types of beverages, amounts consumed, frequencies, and so forth. In so far as the phrase college drinking suggests any such patterns—and we saw in Chapter 3 that it does to many people—it is misleading. Not only is no single pattern dominant, but the suggestion that the drinking largely occurs in the physical structure, the grounds and buildings, which the word college immediately brings to mind is erroneous. As Table 57 indicated, only about 3% of the male users reported their college room as the usual place of drinking and less than 3% reported the fraternity or sorority house. Among the women users but 1% reported their room and about 5% the fraternity or sorority house. When it is remembered also that 20% of the men and 39% of the women are abstainers, it can be seen that college buildings and grounds are hardly the scene of a well-developed pattern of drinking. Most drinking by college students takes place in homes, or public places such as restaurants, taverns, bars or night clubs. The clumsy title, Drinking Habits and Attitudes of Those Enrolled in College would most accurately describe the phenomena we have been studying.

Interpreted in the strict sense, no such pattern as college drinking or drinking in college exists.

We have suggested that beer drinking in all-male groups is more common during college than later on. It may be more common for college men than for other men of the same age, although we do not have evidence on this. Such drinking was frequent in the German and English universities of the 19th century which strongly influenced our universities in other respects. Certainly this sort of drinking is by no means representative of college drinking in general. Although beer is the most usual alcoholic drink for 72% of the men, it must be remembered that many of these prefer wine or spirits to beer. Also much beer drinking takes place at home, in mixed company, alone, or with one other person. Clearly then, beer drinking in all-male groups is but one of many patterns among the male drinkers; and since women drinkers do not display this behavior at all, it certainly cannot be considered the typical mode of college drinking. In addition, any stereotype of wild or heavy drinking applied to college students is utterly unreal in so far as the evidence from these colleges and students is concerned. Including additional colleges and students would not be likely to change this conclusion.

That post-childhood drinking ordinarily starts for the student drinkers before they get to college is abundantly clear. Four-fifths of the male student drinkers and two-thirds of the females began to drink before they came to college. More than half of all the male users and two-thirds of the women users report (Table 54) that their first post-childhood drinking took place in their own home (34% of the men, 53% of the women) or in the home of a friend (17% of the men, 14% of the women).

For the great majority of college students drinking does not start in college, does not take place within the college, and shows no dominant collegiate pattern. With these facts in mind it is possible to consider the matter of drinking and the colleges with some degree of realism. Of the college students who drink, about half had adopted the custom by the age of 17, most of them starting at 16 or 17 (Table 53). Although their drinking begins shortly before or at the time they enter college, the fact of being in college appears to have little influence on this behavior. The process of growing up

seems to be a far more significant factor in drinking than admission
to a college. Growing up refers here in only a minor sense to
chronological age or physical development. Primarily it covers
sociological changes common to those in the late teens in most
strata of American life: a variety of changes in role, increasing independence of parental authority, extension of the friendship group,
and the like. The armed forces, employers of late adolescents, and
the community itself face almost the same problems in relation to
drinking among those of this age group as do the colleges. The
differences are not in the drinking but in the responsibilities and
goals of colleges, which are distinct or different in degree from
those of the community, the armed services, employers, or others.

Whether they like it or not, the colleges bear more responsibility
than other groups for the general behavior of the young men and
women who attend them. Unlike employers, religious leaders or
high school teachers, who have responsibilities for young people
only at a particular time, in a particular place, or for a particular
purpose, college administrators are often held responsible for the
total behavior of students at all times and places for the greater
part of four years. As an easily defined and located agency the college cannot avoid such responsibility or pass it on to the family
as community agencies are wont to do. Furthermore most colleges
feel that they cannot, perhaps should not, exert the continuing, detailed, and all-encompassing control over individual behavior
which is considered routine by the armed services and by some
boarding schools.

Extensive responsibility for the general behavior of the students
who happen to have recently adopted the practice of drinking or
are just about to do so has created a specific problem for the colleges. The students who drink are not unlike most of the rest of the
drinking population. This means that some proportion while
drinking will approach the limits of acceptable behavior. It means
that some will get drunk. It means that some, strangely enough the
same proportion as found in the general public, will be approaching or in rare instances may actually have arrived at alcoholism.
But although the proportion of problem behavior or problem be-
havers in college may be similar to that in the general population,
the appearances will be far worse.

Young men and women at college show considerably more physical vigor than do their elders. And they frequently display this vigor in types of behavior which have not been fully learned: often the college boy or girl is away from the scenes and the associations of his earlier years, is undergoing changes in role and activity, and has not yet developed skill, confidence, or perception of the relationship of a particular behavior to his own total behavior or to the interpretation which others will place on it. A certain amount of excessive or nearly deviant behavior may well stem from overshooting the mark in displaying increased independence of parental or similar controls. Whatever the explanations may be, college students and others of like age sometimes act boisterously and with a lack of sensitivity for the rights and feelings of others. With no alcohol at all students can behave on occasion in ways which may suggest intoxication to their elders. They sometimes behave after one small drink as older persons do after several; and when this happens other people, including the college authorities, are likely to attribute it to drinking. When students actually have too many drinks, their behavior may become far more conspicuous than that of older persons would be.

The appearance of a young man or woman is likely to be worse the first time he or she has too much to drink than on the fourth or fifth occasion. However, many of the students who have been tight (about two-thirds of the women and a third of the men according to Table 60) have only had one or two such experiences. Those with signs of incipient alcoholism probably have not yet learned to disguise their behavior like an older incipient alcoholic.

If intoxication is more evident in younger persons than in older ones and is often thought present when it is not, it is easy to see how alarming the signs may appear to be to parents. Unruly behavior of their offspring may be doubly disturbing to them because it occurs away from home (Table 56). How easy to believe that "all this wild drinking" is causally related to the college; it occurs more or less during the years of college. Yet actually, of all the students who had ever been tight, 75% of the men and 47% of the women reported that the first instance occurred away from home but before they went to college.

So it is possible that the colleges are more sensitive to problems actually or apparently related to drinking than the actual facts warrant. And yet the attitudes of parents, of graduates, of people in the city or town where the college is located or in the nearby towns where the students drink must remain very real factors to be considered by college authorities. When these attitudes are taken into account, it is even possible that some of the colleges could be criticized for being undersensitive to the problems. Underlying this mixture of overanxiety and underanxiety will be found the inadequacy and inaccuracy of definition of the phenomenon or problems involved, especially the oversimplification which allows mildly drunken behavior, driving while under the influence of alcohol, drunkenness, alcoholism, and many types of socially acceptable drinking all to be considered as a single phenomenon—even more unrealistically as a phenomenon peculiar to colleges.

Except for those institutions which formally accept a philosophy of total abstinence, the colleges face the same problem with regard to drinking among students as with regard to students' financial expenditures, personal appearance, recreations, sexual behavior, and so on: Shall they censor, guide, or disregard the emerging activities of these near-adults? Their problem may be seen with greater clarity by a comparison with the preparatory schools and postgraduate university schools. In general the preparatory schools can effectively view their students as nonadults and block individual variations or experiments in living, while the postgraduate schools can view their students as adults and disregard responsibilities of this nature, merely expelling a student if his behavior warrants it. But the colleges, no matter what individual parents, faculty members, townspeople, graduates, or students may feel, can rarely if ever adopt such extreme and simple solutions, with a student body ranging in maturity and sophistication from juvenile to adult.

Another important aspect of the situation for the colleges is indicated in the phrase "Colleges have become big business." They have a heavy investment in land, buildings, and personnel (many of whom have "permanent" tenure and retirement rights), and commitments, often of an intangible nature, to past, present, and future students and to society at large. All these will be endangered if those who support the college financially lose confidence in it. These include parents, alumni, legislators, foundations, church groups, the corporations or boards of trustees which manage the college, and other groups or individuals. College administrators are apt to view new or extreme policies of any sort with trepidation, and to look askance at incidents of deviant behavior within the institution; strong policies against drinking of all sorts, extremely lenient policies toward it, and incidents of conspicuously deviant behavior believed to be related to drinking all may jeopardize the confidence that is so necessary to the existence of the organization.

Under the circumstances it is hardly surprising that the general response of the colleges, apart from those in the temperance tradition, to drinking and its problems is like that of other American institutions and groups: to avoid recognition or reaction wherever possible and to develop self-protective and negative responses where necessary.

The exception of the "dry" colleges exists on theoretical grounds only. True, unlike the other colleges they have a formal and clear philosophy, but it is a completely negative one equipped with purely negative responses. A moderate proportion of their students drink, and a fraction of these equal to if not larger than that in the other colleges have drinking problems. It is probable that criticism on the subject by their alumni, boards of directors, and supporting groups and individuals is more severe and upsetting for the "dry" colleges than for any of the others. Any advantage they hold over other colleges is probably balanced by other disadvantages.

Occasionally the problems related to drinking that the colleges face are dramatic and lead to adverse comment in the press, complaints by parents, criticisms from actual or potential sources of funds, and requests for strong action by trustees, students, and others. Ordinarily the policy of college administrators is to set implicit or explicit limits beyond which penalties will be enforced. The range of these limits is broad: one college will expel any student who takes a drink of any alcoholic beverage while within what the college considers its jurisdiction; another will expel or suspend if deviant behavior (whether following drinking or not) attracts adverse publicity. Specific rulings as to when, where, and what are often laid down within these less stringent limits. Enforcement may be spasmodic or fairly continuous. The enforcement personnel exhibit the entire range of possible responses—from actively encouraging such an activity as drinking to applying the severest penalties, from regarding with horror to observing with amusement, from seriously accepting responsibility to evasion and indifference. As in the larger society, actual enforcement is for the most part left to minor functionaries, such as watchmen, campus police, and student monitors, whose major concern may be to "keep the lid on," that is, to achieve a compromise between actual and ideal behavior which will avoid publicity and disturb students and college authorities as little as possible.

The very wide publicity accorded Alcoholics Anonymous, and the marked impact of recent research and clinical work concerned with alcoholism have influenced some colleges to take new steps. It is becoming widely recognized that personality maladjustment is a factor lying behind alcoholism; hence members of the mental hygiene department may be asked not only to be responsible for certain students apparently having difficulties connected with drinking but also to advise on college policy in general on the subject of alcohol. Furthermore, representatives of Alcoholics Anonymous may be invited to speak to classes or special assemblies. It can hardly be questioned that there are benefits to be derived from acquainting students with the work of Alcoholics Anonymous and with the fact that alcoholism is not a hopeless condition. And it is indisputable that personality factors are significant in the development of this illness. But alcoholism is a comparatively unimportant problem on the campus. And these approaches when made alone may even add to the confusion since they do little to discriminate between drinking, drunkenness, and alcoholism and their emphasis is on the most extreme pathologic manifestation of drinking. In this respect they are similar in content though not in motivation to the old temperance talk. These innovations in college activity, it is worth noting, are a reflection of change in the larger society and do not ordinarily involve any radical departure on the part of the colleges from earlier ways.

Is there anything further that the colleges can do which will not result in a clash with that society on whose good will their very existence depends? In our opinion there is a great deal, and they can do it with assurance of resolving more effectively than ever before at least some part of their problems connected with alcohol.

These problems may be classified as two types: those calling for immediate administrative response and those that are educational in nature. On the first level, as we have seen, the colleges have more than ordinary responsibilities and are peculiarly susceptible to criticism. Although newer techniques for handling such matters as alcoholism and drunken driving are becoming available, it is also true that the colleges cannot realistically be asked to move faster than other institutions in the community and society—than government, medicine, the church, industry, and so on. Yet it is not inappropriate to suggest that they should keep abreast of changing concepts and techniques. Furthermore, in applying any techniques of control they will benefit significantly from the realization that there are different sorts of problems and from knowing what they are. Neither Alcoholics Anonymous nor psychiatry is the answer to the usual student problems associated with drinking, any more than religious exhortation or cursing is the answer to alcoholism. For those in the college community who are responsible for the social aspects of student life or are charged with disciplinary duties, and for those engaged in public relations for the college, more knowledge and more effective understanding of alcohol problems is greatly to be desired.

The major contribution of the colleges, however, is to be made in the sphere of education; in the case of the universities, education and research. To date, the subjects of alcohol, drinking, and related problems have for the most part been avoided in the college curriculum. When they have been discussed, it has not been with disciplined objectivity but in the familiar terms and concepts of the 19th-century temperance tradition. Whether the instructors have been sympathetic or antagonistic to the tradition has made little difference since the tradition itself is intellectually inadequate. There has been no alternative "wet" tradition or any other to which they might turn. The so-called Wets have made no constructive contribution to a better understanding of the phenomena or the problems involved. We do not suggest that the colleges should develop a new morality for the society. What we do suggest is that they can and should provide tested knowledge and intellectual training so that their students may meet this aspect of life with greater confidence and more understanding. With such a basis a more mature and integrated approach to the whole question might in time emerge in our society.

It should hardly be necessary to add that the education we are referring to does not involve "teaching students to drink." Alcohol does not appear to do anything for youth which cannot be achieved more effectively and with greater social acceptance in other ways. However, the majority of adults in our society do use alcoholic beverages, and ignorance or misinformation about the subject on the part of user or nonuser has nothing to commend it. Nor does the word education refer here to specialized courses on alcohol or drinking customs. Although these might be appropriate for certain disciplines, it would probably be in advanced courses with emphasis on processes or principles.

One of the purposes of a college education is to equip the student with knowledge, with means of orienting and organizing that knowledge, and with insight into the development, structure, functioning, relationships and meaning of the phenomena he studies. With many students, motivation and ability to learn appear to increase the more directly teaching content relates to their own life experience. This does not mean that an intellectual discipline arises for each object of interest. Over generations or centuries the academic disciplines have developed from studies of this or that specialized topic to comprehension on a more general level which can become relevant to and include whole classes of particular phenomena. We are strongly of the opinion that the phenomena of drinking, as part of the world we live in, are susceptible to analysis by the existing disciplines and are of exceptional interest to college students. Three-quarters of these students participate in the custom of drinking. There is hardly one among them who will not sooner or later have to take a stand on the matter, in several of the various roles of individual, voter, church member, father, worker or employer, neighbor and friend.

The applicability and relevance to academic disciplines of study of the phenomena of alcohol and drinking are extensive: it is pertinent to political science, law, economics, literature, education, psychology, psychiatry, nursing, sociology, chemistry, nutrition, industrial management, and so on. And all of these disciplines can throw light on various aspects of the subject of alcohol and its use. Alcohol is a particularly adaptable vehicle for research since, unlike so many phenomena of intense and widespread human interest, it is a readily identifiable entity; it can serve as an isolated variable for studying human behavior. However, despite its suitability for teaching and research, despite the enormous social problems involved, and despite the great interest of students, disciplined treatment of the subject has been avoided in college teaching and research in the field has been extremely restricted. College instructors to be sure have made extensive remarks on the subject, in texts, lectures, and private conversation. But consciously or unconsciously they have absorbed one or another of the popular attitudes toward it, ordinarily accompanied at certain points with emotion—for college professors are as much members of the culture as are others. And yet their opinions and attitudes do not appear to others to be mere comment by another member of society, but clothed with special wisdom. When instructors' perceptions of the phenomena of alcohol are on a level of broadly oriented, disciplined knowledge, particularly with reference to their own field of specialization, they should be able to deal with the subject not in terms of folk views or superficial action programs but with soundly based objectivity. Applying this knowledge in their own spheres of competence, college faculties should be able to serve a valuable function both in training the intellect and in preparing students for life in their society.

The training students receive before they reach college is important as the basis of their further education. Before 1945 only the most discouraging picture could be given of what was taught about alcohol in high schools and of the possibilities for improvement. It is gratifying to be able to report that in several states there has been a marked change toward more effective teaching since 1947 and, even more significant, that there is evidence of a desire for improvement in many parts of the country.[1] However, the schools in their turn depend upon the colleges, and especially the teachers' colleges. If the subject of alcohol is avoided in the training of schoolteachers, or they are offered narrow viewpoints, misin-

1. Raymond G. McCarthy, "Activities of State Departments of Education concerning Instruction about Alcohol," *Quarterly Journal of Studies on Alcohol 13* (September 1952), 496–511.

formation, or the materials of pressure groups rather than of suitable educational sources, the task of the high schools, which has been well begun, will be made exceedingly difficult.

In order to train youth, teachers must first train themselves. It is our belief that a few members of every faculty, in addition to one or more persons on the administrative level, should become informed about the phenomena of alcohol and drinking, particularly as it pertains to their own field of specialization. Around such an enlightened nucleus in the college a more rational, useful, and appropriate program of education could be expected to develop. The confusion, inconsistency, ignorance, and prejudice so commonly found in our society would not be apt to persist in an academic community where a few well-trained and respected men could be relied on for thorough knowledge and understanding. Such a group might also do research, which would further broaden understanding.

The universities' failure so far to act in these areas, to provide leadership in knowledge and understanding, and to serve as intellectual stimulators and guides to the rest of the educational world obviously does not rise from lack of problems, unavailability of techniques of research or the inapplicability of research to basic knowledge or to related practical and academic fields. It has its source in the intellectual and moral atmosphere which still surrounds the phenomena of alcohol and of drinking in the whole society. But the colleges may change their approach and if they work out more effective solutions of problems, they are likely not only to be accepted but widely copied by the rest of society.

It is our belief that the colleges, together with the high schools and universities, can fulfill a highly significant function in aiding our society to achieve a firmer, more effective, and better integrated morality concerning drinking and its related problems. One of the prerequisites for reaching this goal is to develop well-oriented, disciplined, and relevant knowledge and present it to the younger generation in objective, intelligible, organized, and emotionally meaningful fashion. This the colleges can do appropriately and with competence in so far as they recognize the responsibility and specifically prepare themselves for it.

APPENDIX

List of Items in the Questionnaire

Date
Sex
College year
Major or intended major course of study
Date of birth
Birthplace of self, and of each parent
Dominant nationality background and race of each parent
Place of residence while at college
Number of roommates
Place(s) of residence prior to college
Formal education of each parent
Religious affiliation of self and each parent
Frequency of religious participation (self, each parent)
Marital status
Marital history of parents
If home broken, own age when this occurred
Number of siblings and order of birth
Type(s) of secondary school
Extracurricular activities in college
Paid job at college, if any
Occupation of each parent
Family income and available spending money
For married students, basic background data on spouse
Car available at college
Extent of drinking by self, father, mother, close friends
Instances known of problem drinking

Specific advice given concerning the use of alcoholic beverages

Use of alcoholic beverages before the age of 11

For abstainers only: if ever a user, types of beverage used and time since last use; reasons for abstaining; behavior at affairs where alcohol is served

Age when drinking (beyond childhood drinking) started; before or after entering college

Knowledge and approval or disapproval by parents of early drinking

Place, companions, type of beverage at first drinking (beyond childhood drinking) and when first tight

Age when first tight; with or without knowledge of parents; before or after entering college

Types of beverage, order of preference, and frequency of use

Average amounts consumed at a sitting

Times high, tight, drunk, passed out

Frequency of drinking during past year

Drinking in mixed company

Difference in drinking pattern at college and on vacation

Usual companions and place when drinking beer, wine, spirits

Reasons for drinking

Complications resulting from drinking

Signs of special stress on the importance of drinking

Warning signs of problem drinking

Measures of anxiety over drinking

Attitudes toward drinking by others

Reactions toward abstention in others

Reactions toward drunkenness in others

Opinion about association of drinking with sexual behavior

Reaction toward double standard in drinking

Behavior (associated with drinking) which is "going too far"

Opinion on official college attitude toward drinking

For women, association of drinking with menstrual cycle

Veteran status

For male veterans, drinking patterns during period of service

INDEX

Abstinence: advice regarding, 62–64, 136–137; and anxiety about drinking, 168; attitudes toward, 177–179; reasons for, 64–66; students practicing, 46–47, 175–176, 190–191

Advertising, 127–128

Age of students: by quantity-frequency index, 106; by social complications scale, 159; veterans, 148; when first tight, 108, 134; when postchildhood drinking started, 107–108, 121

Alcohol: as a medicine, 28–29, 30; consumption, historical, 21–26; content in beverages, 86–87, 92, 102; depressant action, 9–12; education about, 15, 34, 58–59, 84, 128–129, 211–214; effects on behavior, 9–12, 22, 103–104, 130–131, 197; per capita consumption, 23–24

Alcoholics Anonymous, 17, 18, 210–211

Alcoholism, 156–157, 170; see also Problem drinking

Americans. See Nationality

Amounts consumed, 101–103, 117; see also Quantity-frequency index

Anticipatory drinkers, 113–114, 139, 151, 162

Anti-Saloon League, 15

Anxiety about drinking, 167–169

Arrests for drunkenness, 16–17

Asbury, Francis, 28

Associated Press, 40

Athletic participation. See Sports

Attitudes about drinking: college administrators 66–69; historical, 26–35; toward Negroes, 32; see also Parents, Stereotypes, Student attitudes

Baird, E. G., 20 n., 27

Beach, F. A., 187 n.

Beer: alcohol content, 86; amounts consumed, 101–103; effects on behavior, 22; historical trends, 21–22, 24; use, general, 23–24; see also Beverages, alcoholic

Beverages, alcoholic: alcohol content, 86–87; amounts consumed, 101–103; cost, 87, 163; nationality, race and religion, 94; quantity-frequency index, 110–111; symbolic values, 87–88; taste, 87, 94; types preferred, 88–99; types used, 77–81, 88–99; use in childhood, 119–120

Blackout, 164–165

Boys, attitude toward drinking by, 173

British. See Nationality

Catholics, 51; see also Churches, Religious affiliation

Childhood drinking, 118–120

Churches, advising abstinence, 62–66, 136–138

College administrators: concern over study, 43–44; policy on drinking, 66–69, 209–210; responsibility of, 206, 211–214

College, as place of drinking, 123, 204–205

College categories: by attitude toward drinking, 175; by incidence of drinking, 47–48; by income of students, 48–49; included in survey, 2–3, 47; not participating in survey, 44

College drinking pattern, 205–206

217

* Since nearly all data are reported according to sex, this differentiation has not been specifically designated in the index except in special cases.